3 0116 00536 0571

Guidance notes and flow charts for the

Term Service Short Contract

This contract should be used for the appointment of a supplier for a period of time to manage and provide a service. The NEC3 Term Service Short Contract is an alternative to the NEC3 Term Service Contract and is for use with contracts which do not require sophisticated management techniques, comprise straightforward work and impose only low risks on both the Employer and the Contractor

An NEC document

April 2013

Construction Clients' Board endorsement of NEC3

The Construction Clients' Board recommends that public sector organisations use the NEC3 contracts when procuring construction. Standardising use of this comprehensive suite of contracts should help to deliver efficiencies across the public sector and promote behaviours in line with the principles of *Achieving Excellence in Construction.*

Facilities Management Board support for NEC3

The Facilities Management Board recognises that the NEC Term Service Contracts support good practice in FM Procurement in the public sector.

Cabinet Office UK

supported by

ADVANCING OUR PROFESSION

NE
NEC3 Term Serv
of Facilities Manageme

D1438601

NEC is a division of Thomas Telford Ltd, which is a wholly owned subsidiary of the Institution of Civil Engineers (ICE), the owner and developer of the NEC.

The NEC is a family of standard contracts, each of which has these characteristics:

- Its use stimulates good management of the relationship between the two parties to the contract and, hence, of the work included in the contract.

- It can be used in a wide variety of commercial situations, for a wide variety of types of work and in any location.

- It is a clear and simple document – using language and a structure which are straightforward and easily understood.

These guidance notes and flow charts are for the Term Service Short Contract which is both part of the NEC family and are consistent with all other NEC3 documents.

ISBN (complete box set) 978 0 7277 5867 5
ISBN (this document) 978 0 7277 5929 0
ISBN (Term Service Short Contract) 978 0 7277 5893 4
ISBN (how to write the TSC Service Information) 978 0 7277 5925 2
ISBN (how to use the TSC communication forms) 978 0 7277 5927 6

First edition 2008
Reprinted 2009, 2010
Reprinted with amendments 2013

British Library Cataloguing in Publication Data for this publication is available from the British Library.

Typeset by Academic + Technical, Bristol

Printed and bound in Great Britain by Bell & Bain Limited, Glasgow, UK

CONTENTS

FOREWORD

I was delighted to be asked to write the Foreword for the NEC3 Contracts.

I have followed the outstanding rise and success of NEC contracts for a number of years now, in particular during my tenure as the 146th President of the Institution of Civil Engineers, 2010/11.

In my position as UK Government's Chief Construction Adviser, I am working with Government and industry to ensure Britain's construction sector is equipped with the knowledge, skills and best practice it needs in its transition to a low carbon economy. I am promoting innovation in the sector, including in particular the use of Building Information Modelling (BIM) in public sector construction procurement; and the synergy and fit with the collaborative nature of NEC contracts is obvious. The Government's construction strategy is a very significant investment and NEC contracts will play an important role in setting high standards of contract preparation, management and the desirable behaviour of our industry.

In the UK, we are faced with having to deliver a 15–20 per cent reduction in the cost to the public sector of construction during the lifetime of this Parliament. Shifting mind-set, attitude and behaviour into best practice NEC processes will go a considerable way to achieving this.

Of course, NEC contracts are used successfully around the world in both public and private sector projects; this trend seems set to continue at an increasing pace. NEC contracts are, according to my good friend and NEC's creator Dr Martin Barnes CBE, about better management of projects. This is quite achievable and I encourage you to understand NEC contracts to the best you can and exploit the potential this offers us all.

Peter Hansford

UK Government's Chief Construction Adviser
Cabinet Office

PREFACE

The NEC contracts are the only suite of standard contracts designed to facilitate and encourage good management of the projects on which they are used. The experience of using NEC contracts around the world is that they really make a difference. Previously, standard contracts were written mainly as legal documents best left in the desk drawer until costly and delaying problems had occurred and there were lengthy arguments about who was to blame.

The language of NEC contracts is clear and simple, and the procedures set out are all designed to stimulate good management. Foresighted collaboration between all the contributors to the project is the aim. The contracts set out how the interfaces between all the organisations involved will be managed – from the client through the designers and main contractors to all the many subcontractors and suppliers.

Versions of the NEC contract are specific to the work of professional service providers such as project managers and designers, to main contractors, to subcontractors and to suppliers. The wide range of situations covered by the contracts means that they do not need to be altered to suit any particular situation.

The NEC contracts are the first to deal specifically and effectively with management of the inevitable risks and uncertainties which are encountered to some extent on all projects. Management of the expected is easy, effective management of the unexpected draws fully on the collaborative approach inherent in the NEC contracts.

Most people working on projects using the NEC contracts for the first time are hugely impressed by the difference between the confrontational characteristics of traditional contracts and the teamwork engendered by the NEC. The NEC does not include specific provisions for dispute avoidance. They are not necessary. Collaborative management itself is designed to avoid disputes and it really works.

It is common for the final account for the work on a project to be settled at the time when the work is finished. The traditional long period of expensive professional work after completion to settle final payments just is not needed.

The NEC contracts are truly a massive change for the better for the industries in which they are used.

Dr Martin Barnes CBE

Originator of the NEC contracts

ACKNOWLEDGEMENTS

The first edition of the NEC Term Service Short Contract was produced by the Institution of Civil Engineers through its NEC Panel. It was mainly drafted by Bill Weddell based on work by Andrew Baird.

The Flow Charts were produced by Ross Hayes.

The original NEC was designed and drafted by Dr Martin Barnes then of Coopers and Lybrand with the assistance of Professor J. G. Perry then of The University of Birmingham, T. W. Weddell then of Travers Morgan Management, T. H. Nicholson, Consultant to the Institution of Civil Engineers, A. Norman then of the University of Manchester Institute of Science and Technology and P. A. Baird, then Corporate Contracts Consultant, Eskom, South Africa.

The members of the NEC Panel are:

N. C. Shaw, FCIPS, CEng, MIMechE (Chairman)
P. A. Baird, BSc, CEng, FICE, M(SA)ICE, MAPM
A. J. M. Blackler, BA, LLB(Cantab), MCIArb
M. Codling, BSc, ICIOB, MAPM
L. T. Eames, BSc, FRICS, FCIOB
M. Garratt, BSc(Hons), MRICS, FCIArb
J. J. Lofty, MRICS

NEC Consultant:

R. A. Gerrard, BSc(Hons), FRICS, FCIArb, FCInstCES

Secretariat:

J. M. Hawkins, BA(Hons), MSc
S. Hernandez, BSc, MSc

AMENDMENTS

Full details of all amendments are available on
www.neccontract.com.

INTRODUCTION

The notes in boxes like this one printed within the NEC Term Service Short Contract (TSSC), explain how to complete TSSC when it is used for a simple, low risk contract. These boxed notes are reproduced in these guidance notes, which also explain the background to the TSSC and give guidance for its use as a main contract. The flow charts show the procedural logic on which the TSSC is based and are published in this volume for reference.

In these guidance notes, as in the contract itself, terms which are defined in the TSSC have capital initials and those which are identified in the Contract Data are in italics. The guidance notes and the flow charts are not part of the TSSC and have no legal function.

WHEN TO USE THE TSSC

Within the NEC family, the TSSC is the alternative to the Term Service Contract (TSC) and is for use with contracts which

- do not require sophisticated management techniques,
- comprise straightforward work and
- impose only low risks on both the *Employer* and the *Contractor*.

Users choosing between the TSSC and the TSC should base their choice purely on the level of complexity of the work required and the level of risk to each of the Parties.

NEC3 contracts

The current list of published NEC3 contracts is stated below:

- NEC3 Engineering and Construction Contract (ECC)
- NEC3 Engineering and Construction Subcontract (ECS)
- NEC3 Engineering and Construction Short Contract (ECSC)
- NEC3 Engineering and Construction Short Subcontract (ECSS)
- NEC3 Professional Services Contract (PSC)
- NEC3 Professional Services Short Contract (PSSC)
- NEC3 Term Service Contract (TSC)
- NEC3 Term Service Short Contract (TSSC)
- NEC3 Supply Contract (SC)
- NEC3 Supply Short Contract (SSC)
- NEC3 Framework Contract (FC)
- NEC3 Adjudicator's Contract (AC)

For general guidance on when to use each contract refer to the NEC3 Procurement and Contract Strategies guide, available on www.neccontract.com.

THE TSSC PACKAGE

The TSSC package includes the conditions of contract and forms which, when filled in (except for the Task Order form), make up a complete contract. The forms are on pages 1 to 9 of the package and are provided for

- the title page and the Contract Forms comprising
- Contract Data
- The *Contractor*'s Offer,
- The *Employer*'s Acceptance,
- Price List,
- Service Information and
- Task Order.

Stage A: How an *Employer* invites tenders for a job

Examples using a fictitious small building job are appended to these notes to illustrate how the title page and Contract Forms should be filled in at each of the following three stages leading to a contract.

The *Employer* uses the package to invite tenders for proposed services by providing the following information on the forms and sending the package to tenderers with the invitation to tender.

- **The title page (page 1) – see example A1**
- **Contract Data (pages 2 & 3) – see example A2**
- **The *Contractor*'s Offer and the *Employer*'s Acceptance (page 4) – leave blank**
- **Price List (page 5) – see notes on clause 50.2**

> The Price List is in two parts. Part 1 is for work described in the Service Information not requiring the *Employer* to issue a Task Order. Part 2 is for work to be carried out within a stated period of time on a Task by Task basis and instructed by Task Order. The Service may comprise work under Part 1 only or Part 2 only or a mix of both.
>
> Entries in the first four columns of Part 1 of the Price List are made either by the *Employer* or the tenderer. Entries in the first four columns of Part 2 of the Price List would normally be made by the *Employer* as the Party most likely to know the kind of work which will be instructed by the issue of Task Orders. The tenderer then enters a rate for each item and multiplies it by the Expected quantity to produce the Price to be entered in the final column.
>
> If the *Contractor* is to be paid an amount for the item which is not adjusted if the quantity of work in the item changes, the tenderer enters the amount in the Price column only, the Unit, Expected quantity and Rate columns being left blank.
>
> If the *Contractor* is to be paid an amount for the item of work which is the rate for the work multiplied by the quantity completed, the tenderer enters a rate for each item and multiplies it by the Expected quantity to produce the Price, to be entered in the final column.
>
> If the *Contractor* is to be paid a Price for an item proportional to the length of time for which a service is provided, a unit of time is stated in the Unit column and the expected length of time (as a quantity of the stated units of time) is stated in the Expected quantity column.

- **Service Information (pages 6–8) (see notes on clauses 11.2(5) and 60.1(1))**

> The Service Information should be a complete and precise statement of the *Employer*'s requirements. If it is incomplete or imprecise there is a risk that the *Contractor* will interpret it differently from the *Employer*'s intention. The Service Information should state clearly the part of the *service* which is to be carried out by the *Contractor* and which does not require the *Employer* to issue a Task Order. This part of the *service* is priced in Part 1 of the Price List. Information provided by the *Contractor* should be listed in the Service Information only if the *Employer* is satisfied that it is required, is part of a complete statement of the *Employer*'s requirements and is consistent with the other parts of the Service Information.

1 Description of the *service*

> Give a detailed description of what the *Contractor* is required to do. This may include drawings.

2 Specifications

> List the specifications that apply to this contract.

It is important that these are thoroughly prepared and comprehensive because the TSSC definition of a Defect (clause 11.2(1)) is based entirely on the Service Information. Include in the specifications details of

- quality standards for design (if any) and workmanship,
- any tests and testing procedures required and
- any specific equipment and methods of construction to be used.

3 Constraints on how the *Contractor* Provides the Service

> State any constraints on the sequence and timing of work and on the methods and conduct of work including the requirements for any work by the *Employer*.

Refer to any specific constraints relating to the country where the *service* is to be provided. These may include provisions such as a labour intensive approach using appropriate technology, and maximising local employment.

The *Contractor* should be allowed to subcontract work without any limit (clause 21.1). However, the *Employer* may wish to limit the extent of subcontracting if, for example, the *Contractor* is being selected for a particular expertise. The *Employer* may also wish to provide lists of subcontractors and suppliers who would be acceptable for specific categories of work or supplies. Any such constraints should be stated here.

If the *Contractor*'s work needs to be co-ordinated with other activities or contracts, define the parts of the *service* affected and state the dates by which each is to be completed.

If the *Contractor*'s work is to be affected by work done by the *Employer*, the nature of the *Employer*'s work, including the timing should be stated.

4 Requirements for the plan

> State whether a plan is required and, if it is, state what form it is to be in, what information is to be shown on it, when it is to be submitted and when it is to be updated.

The plan is an important document for administering the contract. It informs the *Employer* of the *Contractor*'s detailed intentions of how and at what times he is to Provide the Service. It enables the *Employer* to monitor the *Contractor*'s performance and to assess the effects of compensation events.

5 Services and other things provided by the *Employer*

> Describe what the *Employer* will provide, such as services (including water and electricity) and 'free issue' plant, materials and equipment.

The descriptions should include the capacities available and the location of connection points.

Any equipment, information or other things which the *Employer* wishes to take over from the *Contractor* at, or soon after the end of the service period, should be listed (clause 70.2).

6 Property affected by the *service*

> Give information about any property affected by the *service* and any other information which is likely to affect the *Contractor*'s work.

- **Invitation to tender**

The *Employer*'s invitation to tender should include a list of suggested adjudicators from which the tenderers are asked to choose one (see notes on clause 93.2).

The invitation to tender may also include other matters, for example

- any constraints on how the Price List should be used for the submission of tenders,
- if the *Employer* requires tenderers to give names and details of supervisory staff, equipment and methods to be used in Providing the Service, the information should be requested in the invitation to tender (normally, it should be stated that any such details should not form part of the contract and are provided for information only),
- in some circumstances the *Employer* may also wish to draw the attention of tenderers to local employment legislation and health and safety legislation and may also emphasise the importance of gender equality (equal opportunities, equal pay for work of equal value), minimum age of employment and protection of wages (to ensure wages are paid on time and in cash).

Stage B: How a tenderer makes an offer

A tenderer uses the package to make an offer by providing information on the following forms.

- Price List (page 5) – see notes under Stage A and on clause 50.2.
- The *Contractor*'s Offer (page 4) – see example B1

> Enter the total of the Prices from the Price List.

The tenderer's covering letter should also include

- the tenderer's choice of adjudicator from the list suggested by the *Employer* or, if none is acceptable, the tenderer's own suggestions,
- any extra Service Information proposed by the tenderer and

- any additional information asked for by the *Employer* in the invitation to tender, such as
  - names and particulars of tenderer's supervisory staff or workforce proposed and
  - proposals for equipment or methods to be used.

The letter should also make it clear if any part of the *Contractor*'s Offer does not comply with the Contract Data or the Service Information provided by the *Employer*.

Stage C: How a contract is made

The package becomes the complete contract document when the *Employer* makes the following additional entries and sends a copy to the *Contractor* who has made the chosen offer.

- The *Employer*'s Acceptance of the offer (page 4) – see example C1.
- The title page (page 1) – *Contractor*'s name added – see example C2.
- The Contract Forms including the Contract Data (page 3) – *Adjudicator*'s name added – see example C3.

Under the law of England and Wales, the contract between the *Employer* and the *Contractor* is then made. There may be other requirements in other jurisdictions.

The TSSC uses a simple offer (The *Contractor*'s Offer, page 4) and acceptance (The *Employer*'s Acceptance, page 4) to create a contract. It is emphasised that this is the most efficient and clear way of creating a simple contract and users should aim to achieve this. However, if

- the tenderer's covering letter requires changes to the documents (other than to incorporate the addition of the accepted *Adjudicator*) or
- the *Employer* has issued supplements to the invitation to tender amending the documents,

these need to be recorded with the *Contractor*'s Offer or the *Employer*'s Acceptance.

The *Employer* adding into the *Employer*'s Acceptance before this is achieved either by

- the tenderer adding after the offered total of the Prices

  'This offer includes our covering letter

  Reference . . . . Dated . . . . ' or

- the signature

  'The Offer includes the information provided in . . . . '.

(This is either the tenderer's covering letter if not already mentioned in the *Contractor*'s Offer or a document or summary agreed by the two parties after the tender was received.)

NOTES ON THE CLAUSES

1 General

Actions **10**

10.1 This clause obliges the *Employer* and the *Contractor* to do everything which the contract states each of them does. It is the only clause which uses the future tense. For simplicity, everything else is in the present tense.

The requirement that the Parties act 'in a spirit of mutual trust and co-operation' is in accordance with a recommendation of Sir Michael Latham in his report on the UK construction industry ('Constructing the Team', July 1994).

Identified and defined **11**
terms 11.1 The Contract Data is used to complete the contract by identifying terms in italics and providing the information that certain clauses state is in the Contract Data (see examples A2, B1 and C3).

11.2 The meanings of all defined terms are given in this clause.

11.2(1) Any departure from the *service* as specified in the contract constitutes a Defect. This includes departures from the work described in Task Orders as well as departures from the Service Information document.

11.2(2) Defined Cost is defined in this clause in terms of payments made by the *Contractor*. The term is used mainly for assessing certain compensation events (clause 63.2).

11.2(4) Prices may comprise both lump sums and measured items.

11.2(5) One use of this definition of "Provide the Service" in conjunction with the "Service Information" (11.2(6)) is to establish the *Contractor*'s main obligation in clause 20.1.

11.2(6) The Service Information is the *Employer*'s statement of what the *Contractor* is required to do in Providing the Service and what constraints the *Contractor* must comply with (clause 20.1). The Service Information document provided with the invitation to tender will be the basis of the *Contractor*'s tender and must be as comprehensive as possible (see notes on Service Information under 'Stage A: How an *Employer* invites tenders for a job').

The definition includes not only material contained in the document called "Service Information" but also instructions issued under the terms of the contract. This will therefore include Task Orders issued during the course of the contract. The *Employer* may instruct a change to the Service Information document or a Task Order issued under clause 14.6; this may then be a compensation event (clause 60.1(1)).

11.2(7)   The work to be carried out by the *Contractor* in Providing the Service normally consists of two parts.

The first part is the service detailed in the Service Information document and priced in Part 1 of the Price List. The work in this part does not normally require any specific instructions from the *Employer* e.g. sweep the pavements in the High Street four times per day. But other parts of the work may be described in the Service Information document in generic terms since the precise location and timing may not be known at the start of the *service period* e.g. repair potholes in the carriageways. This work may require specific instructions from the *Employer* say, as to location, as and when the work is required. The work so instructed is paid for on a remeasurable basis under Part 1 of the Price List. Such work does not require the detailed instructions including starting and completion dates of the Task Order system.

The second part is the work instructed on a Task by Task basis as and when the *Employer* requires it. These instructions are issued in the form of Task Orders and are priced at the rates and prices in the Price List which contains the expected quantities of such work. Any Task is limited to "work within the *service*". It is important therefore that the "*service*" is drafted in the Contract Data sufficiently widely to include all types of work likely to be instructed by the *Employer* under the system of Task Orders. A Task may be regarded as a "mini-project" which requires greater management in terms of timing, programming and delay damages.

11.2(8)   The specific work comprising a Task Order must have a starting date and a completion date and other information as stated in clause 14.7. A standard Task Order form is included in the contract. The procedure begins with the *Employer* sending to the *Contractor* the instruction which he is proposing to issue. This is priced by the *Contractor* and sent to the *Employer* with the programme he is proposing, to carry out the Task. When the details are agreed, the *Employer* indicates his acceptance and instructs the *Contractor* to carry out the Task.

11.2(9)   The Task Completion Date may be changed when a compensation event occurs affecting the Task.

The Law   12

12.3   Orally agreed changes to the contract have no effect unless they are followed up by the procedures stated in this clause.

Communications   13

13.2   The *period for reply*, stated in the Contract Data (example A2), aims to achieve a timely turn round of communications. Its length depends on the particular circumstances of the contract but would normally be two or three weeks. Other periods for specific actions are stated in the relevant clauses e.g. clause 62.1 – submission of quotations for compensation events. All such periods can be changed only by agreement between the Parties.

The *Employer*'s authority,   14
delegation and   14.1
***Employer*'s Agent**

14.1   Various clauses in the contract give the *Employer* authority to issue instructions to the *Contractor*. These instructions should be given within the limits and for the reasons expressly stated. If for any reason the *Contractor* disagrees with an instruction, having exhausted the procedures in the contract for dealing with such a situation, his remedy is to follow the dispute resolution procedure in clause 93 as appropriate. He should not refuse to obey the instruction.

14.2   Only the *Employer*, or an authorised delegate or agent of the *Employer* (clause 14.4), can change the Service Information or change a Task Order.

	14.3	This clause makes clear that acceptance by the *Employer* of the *Contractor*'s communication or his work does not result in a transfer of liability.
	14.4	Some employers may wish to delegate many of their actions from the start of the contract, for example to an engineer or facilities manager. If this is the case, the instructions to tenderers should state who the expected delegate is and which actions are likely to be delegated.
	14.5	A corporate body may wish to appoint an individual, either from within its own organization or an external consultant to act as its agent under the contract. The *Employer*'s *Agent* may be identified in the Contract Data or appointed some time after the start of the contract.
	14.6	A proposed Task Order is drafted by the *Employer* giving details of the Task and is submitted to the *Contractor* for pricing. The *Contractor* prices the Task Order and submits it to the *Employer* together with a Task Order programme, for the *Employer*'s acceptance. A standard Task Order form is included in the contract.
	14.7	The delay damages to be included in a Task Order are the amount to be paid by the *Contractor* to the *Employer* if the *Contractor* fails to complete the Task by the Task Completion Date. Under the law of England and Wales, the amount of delay damages should not exceed a genuine pre-estimate of the damage that would be suffered by the *Employer* as a result of the delay to completion. The Parties should consult and seek to agree the amount of delay damages for each Task Order.

Employer provides right of **15**
access and things 15.1 &
15.2 — The *Employer* is required to provide the legal right of access to areas affected by the work to be done under the contract. He may not be required to provide the physical access to these areas which may be occupied by people other than the *Employer*. But anything the *Employer* is to provide must be stated in the Service Information, and failure to provide it constitutes a compensation event, clause 60.1(2).

Early warning **16**
16.1 — The obligation which this clause requires of both Parties is intended to bring into the open as early as possible any matter which could adversely affect the successful outcome of the contract. Both Parties should give early warning in order to maximise the time available for taking avoiding action.

16.2 — The Parties are required to co-operate in giving priority to solving the problem, irrespective of how the problem has been caused and who carries financial responsibility for it. Any discussion between the Parties should concentrate on solving the problem. The purpose of the Parties' discussions is not to decide responsibility or who will pay for the actions taken; the relevant provisions of the contract will cover these aspects quite adequately.

2 The *Contractor*'s main responsibilities

Providing the Service **20**
20.1 — This clause states the *Contractor*'s basic obligation. "Provide the Service" is defined in clause 11.2(5). It includes supplying all necessary resources to achieve the end result. It demonstrates the importance of thoroughly prepared and comprehensive Service Information (see notes on Service Information under 'Stage A: How an *Employer* invites tenders for a job').

Subcontracting and people 21

21.1 &
21.2   As in other NEC contracts, the TSSC does not provide for nominated subcontractors. The *Contractor* has full responsibility for Providing the Service, whether subcontracted or not (see notes on Service Information under 'Stage A: How an *Employer* invites tenders for a job').

21.3   The *Employer* has authority to have a *Contractor*'s employee removed from work on the contract. Possible reasons for exercising this authority may include

- security
- health and safety
- disorderly behaviour affecting the *Employer*'s activities.

3 Time

Starting and the   30
service period   30.1   The *starting date* and the *service period* are stated in the Contract Data. If the procurement process and appointment of the *Contractor* takes longer than anticipated, it may be necessary to adjust the *starting date* by agreement before the Contract Date. If a Task Completion Date occurs after the end of the *service period* whether because of the date stated in the Task Order or as a result of a compensation event, the period of the *Contractor*'s obligation to Provide the Service is extended accordingly.

Instructions to stop or not   31
to start work   31.1   This clause gives the *Employer* authority to control the stopping and re-starting of work for any reason, for example, where there is a risk of injury to people or damage to property. An instruction given under this clause constitutes a compensation event (clause 60.1(3)). But if it arises from a fault of the *Contractor*, the Prices are not changed, and in the case of a Task, the Task Completion Date is not changed. In certain circumstances, if the *Employer* fails to instruct the re-start of work within eight weeks of instructing work to stop, the *Contractor* may be entitled to terminate (clause 90.4).

The *Contractor*'s plan   32
32.1   The *Employer*'s requirements for the *Contractor*'s plan should be stated in the Service Information (see notes on Service Information under 'Stage A: How an *Employer* invites tenders for a job'). Some Employers may require tenderers to submit a plan with their tenders. The *Contractor*'s plan is an important document for administering the contract. It informs the *Employer* of the *Contractor*'s detailed intentions of how he is to Provide the Service. It enables the *Employer* to monitor the *Contractor*'s performance and to assess the effects of compensation events.

4 Testing and Defects

Tests and inspections 40

40.1 The Service Information should include a comprehensive specification of the standards to be achieved for both work and materials.

Any specific requirements of the *Employer* for inspection and testing should be stated in the Service Information, including the associated procedures and responsibilities for carrying out the tests (see notes on Service Information under 'Stage A: How an *Employer* invites tenders for a job').

Where payment for work on its completion is dependent on a test being successful, the description of the item in the Price List should include a reference to the test stated in the Service Information. Where appropriate, separate items may be included in the Price List for carrying out tests which are the *Contractor*'s responsibility.

Notifying Defects 41

41.1 The definition of a Defect (clause 11.2(1)) is based entirely on the Service Information which includes Task Orders. If the *Employer* is not satisfied with work for a reason other than that it is not in accordance with the Service Information or Task Order, the work would not be a Defect. In order to 'correct' the work, the *Employer* would need to instruct a change to the Service Information or Task Order, and this would be a compensation event (clause 60.1(1)).

Correcting Defects 42

42.1 There is no fixed time within which the *Contractor* is required to correct a Defect or make good an omission. This will depend on the circumstances of each particular case. The test to be applied in each case is "Within what time will the Defect or omission and its correction or making good, cause the minimum adverse effect on the *Employer* or others?"

Accepting Defects 43

43.1 Although a Defect may be minor, its correction may be costly to the *Contractor*. Correction of the Defect may also cause inconvenience to the *Employer* out of all proportion to the benefits gained. Correction of the Defect may even have become impossible because of the passage of time or some other reason. This clause states a procedure within the contract for accepting a Defect in these circumstances. Either the *Contractor* or the *Employer* may propose that the Defect should be accepted. The other is not obliged to accept the proposal.

The *Contractor*'s quotation will show a reduction to the Prices. In some cases the reduction may be nominal. If the quotation is not accepted by the *Employer* no further action is necessary other than correction of the Defect.

5 Payment

Assessing the amount due   **50**

50.1   The *Employer*'s statement in the Contract Data fixes an *assessment day* in each month from the *starting date* until the month after the later of the end of the *service period* and the latest date for completion of a Task. This provides for a monthly assessment by the *Contractor* even when the amount due may be nil.

The *Contractor* assesses the amount due by each *assessment day* and uses the assessment to apply to the *Employer* for payment. The "amount due" is the total payment due to date. The *Contractor*'s application for payment is for the change in the amount due since the last payment.

50.2   The payment mechanism is largely based on the use of the Price List and the Prices.

The Price List included in the contract provides the pricing information needed for assessing the amount due. Notes on how to use the Price List are included under its heading in the TSSC and are repeated in these notes under 'Stage A:

How an *Employer* invites tenders for a job'.

The Prices are defined in clause 11.2(4). The second sentence of the definition provides for the pricing of those items for which a quantity and a rate are stated in the Price List.

Payments for an item in the Price List do not become due until the work described in the item has been completed unless a quantity and a rate are stated, in which case only the Price for the quantity of work completed is included.

Part 1 of the Price List provides for flexibility in tendering methods including items which

  a) the *Employer* describes and for which the tenderer quotes a Price,
  b) the *Employer* describes with a quantity and for which the tenderer quotes a rate extended to a Price (adjustable to quantity completed),
  c) the *Employer* describes and the tenderer breaks down into sub-items comprising a mixture of a) and b), each of which the tenderer quotes for,
  d) the *Employer* describes and the tenderer quotes for a list of the activities necessary to complete the item, each with a Price, or
  e) the tenderer describes and quotes Prices or rates in accordance with the notes at the head of the Price List and the invitation to tender.

The *Employer* should include in the invitation to tender any constraints on how the Price List should be used for the submission of tenders.

It is important that item descriptions are carefully written with appropriate references to the Service Information, including testing requirements. For measured items, the work to be covered by the rate must be clearly stated. If there is a risk of differing interpretations on how an item is measured, the basis of measurement should be included in the item description of the Price List.

The fourth and fifth bullets in clause 50.2 refer to other amounts to be added or deducted in order to calculate the amount due. Amounts added may include interest on late payments and deductions may include such things as delay damages.

It is recommended that the Parties should agree, at the start of the contract, how the administration of sales tax documentation should be dealt with as part of the payment procedure.

No provision is made for inflation. In some countries where inflation is high the *Employer* may wish to take the risk of price increases beyond a predetermined threshold. This could be provided for in additional conditions of contract.

No provision has been made for advanced payments. If the *Employer* is prepared to make an advanced payment, a separate item should be included in the Price List. The item must describe how the advanced payment is repaid.

This clause should be read in conjunction with clause 51.2 with respect to late payments.

50.3 If the Housing Grants, Construction and Regeneration Act (1996), as modified by the Local Democracy, Economic Development and Construction Act 2009 (the Act), applies to the work in the contract clause 50.3 is amended and further payment provisions added by the additional clauses 1.1 to 1.3, to make the payment procedures comply with the Act. Guidance on these can be found later in these Guidance Notes.

Payment 51

51.1 The latest date for payment is related to the assessment day which occurs after the *Employer* receives the *Contractor*'s application.

51.2 For simplicity, a fixed rate of interest of 0.5% per week is stated for the calculation of interest due on late payments, with an option for the *Employer* to state a different rate in the Contract Data.

> Insert a rate only if a rate less than 0.5% per week of delay has been agreed

6 Compensation events

Compensation events 60 As in other NEC contracts, compensation events are those events stated in the contract to be compensation events. If an event is not so stated, it is not a compensation event and is at the *Contractor*'s financial risk. If a compensation event occurs and does not arise from the *Contractor*'s fault, the *Contractor* may be compensated for any effect the event has on cost or in the case of a Task, on the Task Completion Date.

60.1 Events which are compensation events in the TSSC are listed in this clause. Any additional compensation events required for a particular contract should be stated in an additional condition of contract in the Contract Data.

60.1(1) This clause embodies the principle that a tender can only be based on the information the tenderer has when the tender is prepared. The exception is the case when the *Employer* is willing to accept a Defect and has agreed to change the Service Information to accommodate it. Service Information as defined in clause 11.2(6) comprises the document called "Service Information" together with any instructions issued under the contract. The latter include Task Orders. Hence a change to a Task Order is a compensation event under this clause.

60.1(2) This relates to the *Employer*'s obligation in clause 15.1 to provide the necessary right of access. It also includes the failure of the *Employer* to provide other things as stated in the Service Information (clause 15.2).

60.1(3) This clause relates to the *Employer*'s authority in clause 31.1 to stop or not to start work.

60.1(4)   This relates to the *Employer*'s obligation in clause 13.2 to reply to a communication within stated periods.

60.1(5)   The *Employer* is able to change a decision made under the contract.

Any compensation events other than those identified in clause 60.1 that are required for a specific contract should be stated in an additional condition of contract in the Contract Data. For example, if there is a significant risk of an increase in the cost of labour due to changes in the law, the occurrence of such a change could be made a compensation event. Any risk which it is prudent for the *Employer* to carry can be dealt with in this way.

60.1(6)   The first part of this compensation event deals with the failure of the *Employer* to comply with a Task programme. Therefore the *Employer* needs to check carefully the relevant dates in any Task programme the *Contractor* submits. The second part deals with a situation where the Service information gives details of the order and timing of works by the *Employer*, and he fails to meet those requirements.

60.1(7)   The *Employer* has the right to change a Task Order in the same way that he can change he can change the Service Information, as set out in clause 14.2.

Notifying compensation **61**
events **61.1**   Either the *Employer* or the *Contractor* can notify a compensation event to the other; this clause limits when the *Contractor* can do so. The *Employer* would normally instruct the *Contractor* to submit a quotation at the same time as notifying the *Contractor* of a compensation event.

The stated time limit is intended to expedite the procedure so that dealing with compensation events a long time after they have occurred is avoided.

61.2   This clause states the actions to be taken by the *Employer* within one week of a compensation event being notified by the *Contractor*. If the *Employer* decides that a notified event is not a compensation event, the compensation event procedure does not continue. The *Contractor* may then decide to refer the decision to the *Adjudicator*.

Quotations for **62**
compensation events **62.1**   This clause describes what a quotation for a compensation event is to comprise and states the periods within which the *Contractor* is required to submit it. Where a compensation event affects a Task Completion Date in that it is critical to the programmed completion of the Task, the *Contractor* should include in his quotation an appropriate revised Task Completion Date.

62.2   If the *Contractor* fails to provide a quotation within two weeks, as is required by clause 62.1, the *Employer* notifies his own assessment of the compensation event. In that case if the *Contractor* is dissatisfied with the assessment he refers it to the *Adjudicator*.

Assessing compensation **63**   Clause 63 states how the effects of compensation events on the Prices are
events   assessed. This is the same whether the assessment is done by the *Contractor*, the *Employer* or the *Adjudicator*.

63.1   This clause describes the assessment procedure used when the compensation event affects only the quantities of work to be done under items in the Price List for which a quantity and rate are stated. For simplicity, the rates in the Price List are used to price the changed quantities.

63.2   This clause states the procedure used for all other compensation events. The effect of the compensation event on cost is assessed either as recorded, for work already done or as forecast for work yet to be done.

The percentages for overheads and profit quoted in the *Contractor*'s Offer (see notes on 'Stage B: How a tenderer makes an offer' and example B1) are applied to any change in cost due to the compensation event. Each percentage is required to cover all costs and overheads not included in cost as well as an allowance for profit. One percentage is applied to all elements of cost except people. A separate percentage is used for people because this may be at a different level.

63.3 If the *Contractor*'s planned completion of a Task is delayed by the forecast effect of a compensation event, the Task Completion Date is delayed by the same period.

63.4 The cost of preparing quotations for a compensation event is specifically excluded from the assessment of that compensation event. The *Contractor* should therefore allow for these costs in his percentages for overheads and profits he quotes in the *Contractor*'s Offer in the Contract Data.

63.5 The value of compensation events are added to the Price List.

63.6 This clause emphasises the finality of the assessment of compensation events. If the forecast of the effect on cost included in the accepted or notified assessment proves to be wrong when the work is done, the assessment is not changed.

7 Use of equipment and things

The Parties' use of equipment and things 70

70.1 This clause prohibits the *Contractor* from using equipment and other things provided by the *Employer* for his own purposes or for purposes other than for Providing the Service.

70.2 This requires the *Contractor* to return to the *Employer* at the end of the *service period* or a later date for completion of a Task, things which have been provided by the *Employer* for the *Contractor*'s use. If the Service Information so states, the *Employer* may take over from the *Contractor* at the end of the *service period* or later date for completion of a Task, things belonging to the *Contractor* which he has used to Provide the Service.

8 Indemnity, insurance and liability

The method of dealing with the *Employer*'s and *Contractor*'s risks used in the TSSC is different to the approach in the TSC.

The *Contractor*'s liability to Provide the Service is stated in the TSSC in clause 20.1. Certain financial risks, however, constitute compensation events in clause 60.1. Additional conditions of contract stated in the Contract Data may include further compensation events.

Limitation of liability 80 This clause deals with the aspects of liability which concern contractors most.

80.1 This concerns the *Contractor*'s liability for loss of and damage to the *Employer*'s property. This would normally be unlimited unless a limit is set as required by this clause. The amount stated in the Contract Data is generally set at not more than the cover provided by the insurance required in terms of the contract. In effect, the *Contractor* is then only exposed to the amount of the deductible for any one claim.

80.2 This clause limits the *Contractor*'s exposure to what are commonly referred to as consequential or indirect losses incurred by the *Employer*.

Insurance cover 82

82.1 The *Contractor*'s responsibility for providing insurances is stated in this clause, which includes the Insurance Table. The duration of insurance cover is from the *starting date* until the end of the *service period* or the latest date for completion of a Task whichever is the later. It is suggested that at the start of the contract the *Contractor* advises his insurer of the possibility that the duration of insurances may need to be extended to cover Tasks which may not be completed until the end of the *service period*.

If the date for completion of a Task is later than the end of the *service period* it is essential that the *Contractor* notifies the insurer accordingly at the time to ensure that the proper insurance cover is in place. This situation may arise as a result of a Task Completion Date or of actual completion of a Task, being later than the end of the *service period*, or of a compensation event affecting a Task which in turn results in an extension of its Completion Date.

The *Employer* is required to state in the Contract Data the extent of the insurances the *Employer* is providing (if any) and the minimum amount of cover for the first, third and fourth insurances in the Insurance Table.

Insurance of equipment is on a value indemnity basis. This is particularly relevant to insurance of equipment as it means that cover is for replacement with equipment of similar age and condition rather than on a "new for old" basis.

With regard to the fourth event in the Insurance Table, employers in many countries are required by law to insure employees for personal injury and death.

The *Employer* should ensure that policies are in joint names including for those insurances procured by the *Employer* for those matters at the *Employer*'s risk.

9 Termination and dispute resolution

Termination and reasons for termination 90

90.1 Both the *Employer* and *Contractor* have rights to terminate the *Contractor*'s obligations under the contract in certain circumstances. This termination does not terminate the contract itself. The *Employer* is obliged to issue a termination certificate if either Party wishes to terminate in accordance with clauses 90.2, 90.3, 90.4 or 90.5. The *Contractor* then does no further work.

90.2 to 90.5 The *Employer* may terminate for any reason (clause 90.3). The *Contractor* may terminate only for the particular reasons stated.

Procedures on termination 91

91.1 The *Employer* will secure title to any materials when the *Employer* has paid for them. This will be achieved by the payment on termination (see clause 92.1). The *Contractor* is required to remove his equipment.

Payment on termination 92

92.1 This clause lists the components that are always included in the amount due on termination.

92.2 & 92.3 These clauses state further components which are included in the amount due when termination has occurred for particular reasons. They reflect the different reasons for termination.

Reason 8 is deliberately not mentioned in these clauses. If Reason 8 is the cause of termination the amount due is only that stated in clause 92.1.

Dispute resolution 93   The simple adjudication procedure provided is designed to be appropriate for the type of work likely to be undertaken under the TSSC. If the Housing Grants, Construction and Regeneration Act (1996), as modified by the Local Democracy, Economic Development and Construction Act 2009 (the Act), applies to the work in the contract the clauses in this section are changed and supplemented by the additional clauses 1.4 to 1.8, to make the dispute resolution procedures comply with the Act. Guidance on these can be found later in these Guidance Notes.

93.1   This clause establishes the principle, followed in other NEC contracts, that any dispute which cannot be resolved by the Parties themselves must be decided by the *Adjudicator* who is independent of the Parties and is required to act impartially.

It is important for the Parties to understand that both dispute resolution processes should only be used after attempts at negotiations have failed. They should not be seen as an alternative to the Parties reaching agreement on their disputes, either through informal negotiation, or via other more formal non-binding processes such as mediation or conciliation. Such negotiations will usually need to take place within a short time period because of the limited time available to refer a dispute to the *Adjudicator* in clause 93.3(1). However the Parties can change the contract to extend this time limit by an agreement recorded in accordance with clause 12.3, if they feel that more time is needed for resolving the dispute. If the referral is not made within the time stated or if that time is not extended by agreement, the Parties may no longer dispute the matter. In the UK, if the Act applies to this contract, clause 93.3(1) does not apply, and the substituted clauses allow a dispute to be referred to the *Adjudicator* at any time. Therefore the Parties may take the time they wish to attempt to reach agreement.

The *Adjudicator* 93.2(1)   The person appointed as *Adjudicator* should normally be named in the Contract Data. The *Adjudicator*'s impartiality and independence must be ensured. It is recommended that possible names are suggested by the *Employer* in the invitation to tender so that the *Contractor* can agree a name for inclusion in the final Contract Data (see examples A2 and C3). Acceptance of the *Contractor*'s Offer signifies agreement to the named *Adjudicator*.

The *Adjudicator* should be a person with practical experience of the kind of service to be provided by the *Contractor*. The *Adjudicator* should be able to

- understand the procedures embodied in the TSSC
- understand the roles of both the *Employer* and the *Contractor* in the TSSC
- act impartially and in a spirit of independence of the Parties
- understand and have access to costs at current market rates
- understand and have access to information on planning times and productivities
- appreciate risks and how allowances for them should be set and
- obtain other specialist advice when required.

93.2(2)   This clause makes provision for the appointment of an *Adjudicator* when necessary. This will be because one was not identified in the Contract Data, or the originally chosen *Adjudicator* is no longer able to act. Initially, the Parties should try to reach agreement on a suitable person. If they cannot agree, the *Adjudicator nominating body* named in the Contract Data will make the choice for them. In the UK, the Construction Industry Council and the professional institutions have lists of adjudicators from which the *Adjudicator* may be selected.

The adjudication	93.3(1)	In order to ensure the early declaration of a dispute and expedite its resolution, time limits are stated. After notification of a dispute a minimum of two weeks (maximum four weeks) has to elapse before the dispute can be referred to the *Adjudicator*. This is intended to allow and encourage the Parties to resolve the dispute themselves. Compliance with the time periods stated in this clause is crucially important otherwise the dispute is barred from referral to the *Adjudicator*.

If the Housing Grants, Construction and Regeneration Act (1996), as modified by the Local Democracy, Economic Development and Construction Act 2009, applies to the work in the contract this clause is replaced with one set out in the additional clause 1.5. Guidance on this can be found later in these Guidance Notes.

	93.3(2) & (3)	These clauses set time limits for providing information to the *Adjudicator,* and allow the *Adjudicator* to issue any instructions necessary to help him in reaching a decision.
	93.3(5)	This requires the *Adjudicator* to use the procedures for assessing compensation events in clause 63 if he has to assess additional cost or delay caused to the *Contractor*.
	93.3(6)	The time for the *Adjudicator*'s decision is fixed, but it can be extended if necessary by agreement. If the decision is not given within the time required, and no further time is agreed, a Party can act as though the *Adjudicator* had resigned. This allows the Party to have a replacement *Adjudicator* appointed under clause 93.2(2).
Review by the *tribunal*	93.4	Under clause 93.3(8) the *Adjudicator*'s decision is binding unless and until it is revised by the *tribunal*. A dispute cannot be referred to the *tribunal* unless it has first been referred to the *Adjudicator*.

This clause states the circumstances in which a referral can be made with a time limit for notifying a Party's intention to do so. The *Employer* identifies the *tribunal* in the Contract Data (see example A2). The choice will normally be between arbitration and the courts, either being competent to give a legally final and binding decision on the dispute. It is important to be aware of the different choices that are available when making the decision about the *tribunal*. Different laws and arbitration procedures exist in different countries, whilst in some countries no arbitration exists at all. If the *tribunal* is arbitration, the arbitration procedure to be used is also stated in the Contract Data (see example A2).

The Housing Grants, Construction and Regeneration Act 1996		If the Housing Grants, Construction and Regeneration Act (1996), as modified by the Local Democracy, Economic Development and Construction Act 2009, (the Act) applies to the work in the contract the *Employer* should signify so in the relevant entry on Page 2 of the Contract Data and clauses 1.1 to 1.8 will apply. These add to and change the payment and dispute resolution provisions set out in the rest of the contract.

Much of the works carried out under the TSSC will not fall within the ambit of the Act. However the definition of what activities and contracts the Act applies to is complex, and, if the *Employer* is unsure, it is recommended that legal advice is obtained as to whether or not the Act applies.

	1.1	In order to comply with Section 110 of the Act, this clause defines when the payment becomes due and the final date for payment.
	1.2	This clause confirms that the *Contractor*'s application, issued in accordance with clause 50.1, is the notice of payment required by Section 110A of the Act. It is required to show the basis upon which any payment due has been calculated.

1.3   This clause replaces clause 50.4 of the contract.

In order to comply with Section 111 of the Act it sets out the requirement that, if the *Employer* wishes to pay less than the sum set out the *Contractor*'s application, he must give a notice setting out the amount he intends to pay and the basis upon which it has been calculated. This notice must be given at least 7 days before the final date for payment set out in clause 1.1(2). Without such notice the *Employer* is required to pay the sum in the *Contractor*'s application.

1.4   Under Section 112 of the Act the *Contractor* has the right to suspend performance of all or any part of the *services* if

- he is not paid the amount set out in his application-by the final date for payment, unless a notice to pay a lesser sum has been given in accordance with clause 1.3, or
- if a notice to pay a lesser sum has been given in accordance with clause 1.3, and that lesser sum has not been paid by the final date for payment.

If the *Contractor* exercises this right it is a compensation event.

1.5   This clause replaces clause 93.3(1). It allows for adjudication to take place at any time, as required by the Act, rather than within the strict time limits set out in clause 93.3(1).

1.6   This clause gives the *Adjudicator* the power to decide how to allocate his fees and expenses between the Parties. This clause, which is required by the Act, means that the Parties have agreed to implement the provision in the NEC Adjudicator's Contract allowing the Parties to agree that these fees and expenses will not be shared equally.

1.7   Once the *Adjudicator* has made his decision and notified it to the Parties his role in the dispute would normally be over. This clause gives him the right to subsequently correct a clerical or typographical error which has arisen by accident or by omission, as is required by the Act.

JOINING SUBCONTRACT DISPUTES WITH MAIN CONTRACT DISPUTES

The following notes apply only if the Housing Grants, Construction and Regeneration Act 1996, as modified by the local Democracy, Economic Development and Construction Act 2009, does not apply.

Under clause 21.1, the *Contractor* is responsible for all subcontractors. It is recommended that the *Adjudicator* named in the main contract is also appointed to act in all subcontracts, subject, of course, to the agreement of the subcontractor concerned.

If the *Contractor* wishes to have any matter arising under or in connection with a subcontract that impinges on a main contract matter decided with the main contract matter, the following clause should be included in the main contract.

Combining procedures 93.5   If there is a matter arising under or in connection with a subcontract to this contract which is also a matter arising under or in connection with this contract

- the *Contractor* notifies the subcontractor that the subcontractor may attend the meeting between the Parties or
- the *Contractor* may submit the subcontract matter to the *Adjudicator* at the same time as the main contract matter.

Decisions are made on the two matters together and references to the Parties include the subcontractor.

Stage A   How an *Employer* invites tenders for a job

Example A1   Title page

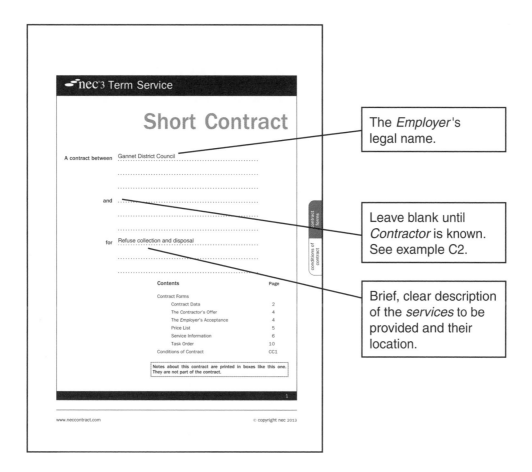

Example A2   Contract Data

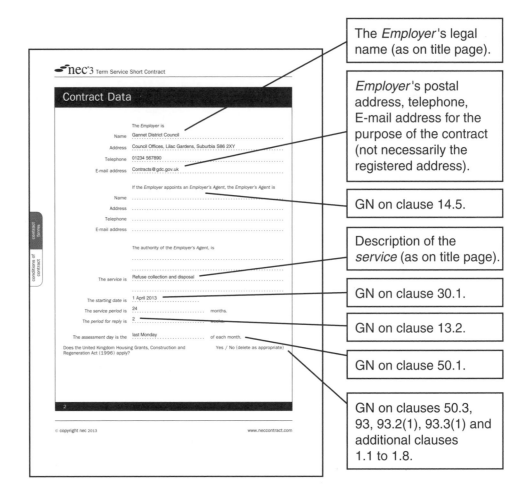

The *Employer*'s legal name (as on title page).

Employer's postal address, telephone, E-mail address for the purpose of the contract (not necessarily the registered address).

GN on clause 14.5.

Description of the *service* (as on title page).

GN on clause 30.1.

GN on clause 13.2.

GN on clause 50.1.

GN on clauses 50.3, 93, 93.2(1), 93.3(1) and additional clauses 1.1 to 1.8.

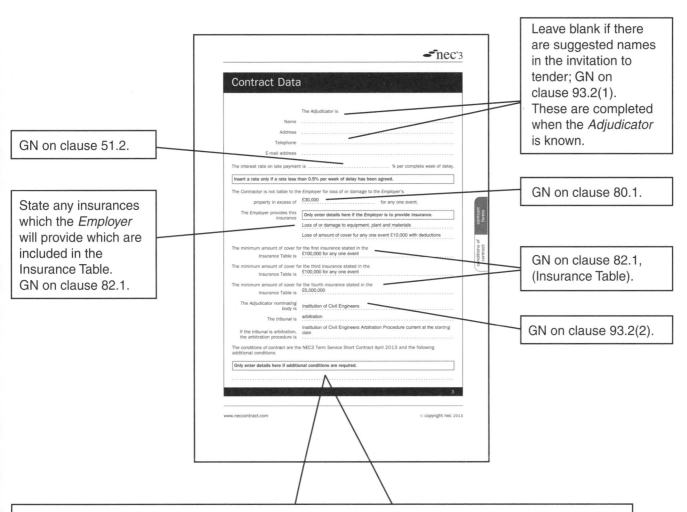

Leave blank if there are suggested names in the invitation to tender; GN on clause 93.2(1). These are completed when the *Adjudicator* is known.

GN on clause 51.2.

State any insurances which the *Employer* will provide which are included in the Insurance Table. GN on clause 82.1.

GN on clause 80.1.

GN on clause 82.1, (Insurance Table).

GN on clause 93.2(2).

If the *Employer* requires to include additional conditions of contract they should be inserted in the box provided at the end of the Contract Data. Any additional conditions should be drafted in the same style as the TSSC clauses, using the same defined terms and other terminology. They should be carefully checked, preferably by flowcharting, to ensure that they mesh with the TSSC clauses.

Additional conditions should be used only when absolutely necessary to accommodate special needs which are not covered by the TSSC clauses. Such special needs may be those peculiar to the country where the work is to be done.

See notes on additional compensation events under clause 60.1.

Many special needs can be accommodated during the invitation to tender, by insertions in the Works Information and by appropriate use of the Price List.

Stage B How a tenderer makes an offer

Example B1 The *Contractor*'s Offer

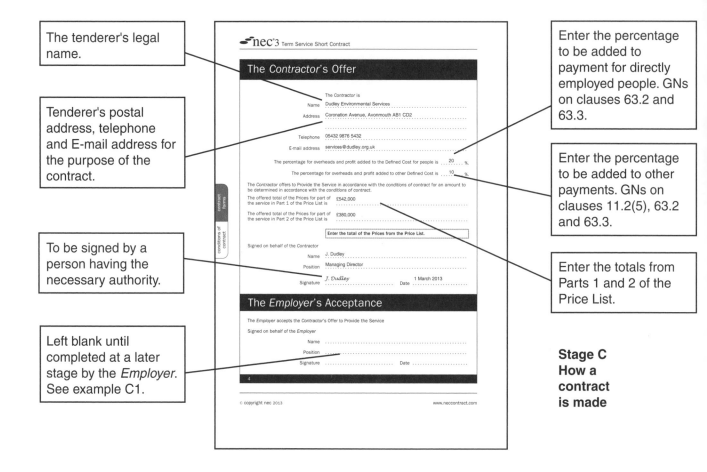

The tenderer's legal name.

Tenderer's postal address, telephone and E-mail address for the purpose of the contract.

To be signed by a person having the necessary authority.

Left blank until completed at a later stage by the *Employer*. See example C1.

Enter the percentage to be added to payment for directly employed people. GNs on clauses 63.2 and 63.3.

Enter the percentage to be added to other payments. GNs on clauses 11.2(5), 63.2 and 63.3.

Enter the totals from Parts 1 and 2 of the Price List.

**Stage C
How a
contract
is made**

Stage C How a contract is made

Example C1 The *Employer*'s acceptance

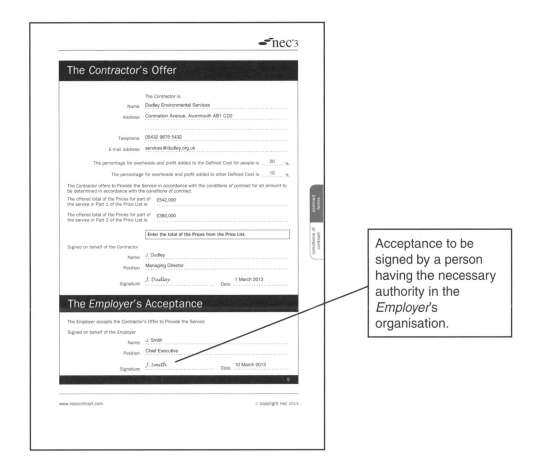

Example C2   Title page

Example C3   Contract Data

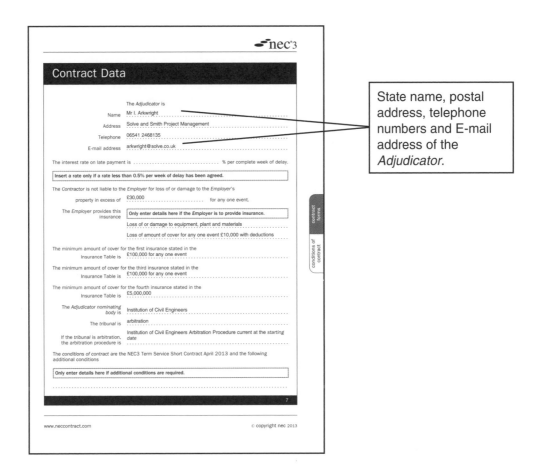

MULTI-PARTY PARTNERING

Introduction

A partnering contract, between two Parties only, is achieved by using a standard NEC contract. If partnering is required between two or more parties working on the same project or programme of projects, then amendments are required to the TSSC. In other NEC contracts, secondary Option X12 Partnering is provided to achieve this arrangement. The TSSC does not have a secondary Options structure so a stand alone clause has been drafted using X12 as a basis. This stand alone clause is referred to as the TSSC multi-party partnering clause in this document. This clause can be used alongside other contracts using X12. Similar amendments would be necessary if the multi-party arrangement was to be extended to a subcontractor appointed using the TSSC as a subcontract.

The parties who have the TSSC multi-party partnering clause included in their contracts are all the bodies who are intended to make up the project partnering team. The TSSC multi-party partnering clause does not create a multi-party contract.

This clause does not duplicate provisions of the appropriate existing conditions of contract in the NEC family that will be used for the individual contracts. It follows normal NEC structure in that it is made up of clauses, data and information.

The content is derived from the Guide to Project Team Partnering published by the Construction Industry Council (CIC). The requirements of the CIC document that are not already in the NEC bi-party contract are covered in this clause. The structure of the NEC family of contracts means the TSSC multi-party partnering clause will not work unless an NEC contract is used.

The purpose of this clause (and Option X12 Partnering) is to establish the NEC family as an effective contract basis for multi-party partnering. As with all NEC documents it is intended that the range of application should be wide. By linking this clause (or X12) to appropriate bi-party contracts, it is intended that the NEC can be used for partnering for any number of projects (i.e. single project or multi-project),

- internationally,
- for projects of any technical composition, and
- as far down the supply chain as required.

This clause is given legal effect by including it in the appropriate bi-party contract. It is not a free standing contract but a part of each bi-party contract that is common to all contracts in a project team.

The underlying bi-party contract will be for a contribution of any type, the work content or objective of which is sufficiently defined to permit a conventional NEC contract to be signed.

Parties must recognise that by entering into a contract with the TSSC multi-party partnering clause they will be undertaking responsibilities additional to those in the basic NEC contract.

A dispute (or difference) between Partners who do not have a contract between themselves is resolved by the Core Group. This is the Group that manages the conduct of the Partners in accordance with the Partnering Information. If the Core Group is unable to resolve the issue, then it is resolved under the procedure of the Partners' Own Contracts, either directly or indirectly with the *Client*, who will always be involved at some stage in the contractual chain. The *Client* may seek to have the issues on all contracts dealt with simultaneously.

The TSSC multi-party partnering clause does not include direct remedies between non-contracting Partners to recover losses suffered by one of them caused by a failure of the other. These remedies remain available in each Partner's Own Contract, but their existence will encourage the parties to compromise any differences that arise.

This applies at all levels of the supply chain, as a *Contractor* who is a Partner retains the responsibility for actions of a subcontractor who is a Partner.

The final sanction against any Partner who fails to act as stated in the TSSC multi-party partnering clause is for the Partner who employed them not to invite them to partner again.

Additional Contract Data for the TSSC multi-party partnering clause

The *Client* is the Party for whom the projects are being carried out. He may also be the *Employer* in an NEC contract.

The *Client*'s objective is the objective for the 'programme of projects' if more than one or for 'the project' if only one. The objective should be expressed quantitatively if possible (the business case). It should also include the partnering objectives.

Partnering Information includes any requirements for

- use of common information systems, sharing of offices,
- attendance at Partners' and Core Group meetings,
- participation in partnering workshops,
- arrangements for joint design development,
- value engineering and value management,
- risk management, and
- other matters that the Core Group manages.

This information should not duplicate requirements in the bi-party contracts.

The additional Contract Data for the TSSC multi-party partnering clause, like other Contract Data in the NEC contracts, does not change. The Schedule of Partners and the Schedule of Core Group Members, like the schedules referred to in the Contract Data do change from time to time. The following are samples of the typical information required in these schedules.

Schedule of Partners

Date of last revision: . . . .

The Partners are the following.

Name of Partner	Representative's address and contact details	Contribution and objective	Joining date	Leaving date	Key Performance Indicator	Target	Measurement arrangement	Amount of Payment if the target is improved upon or achieved*

* Enter *nil* in the last column if there is to be no money incentive

Schedule of Core Group Members

Date of last revision: ....

The Core Group members are the *Client* and the following.

Name of Partner	Address and contact details	Joining date	Leaving date

Including the TSSC multi-party partnering clause in the Own Contracts

This clause is given legal effect by including it in the appropriate bi-party contract. It is not a free standing contract but a part of each bi-party contract that is common to all contracts in a project team.

The underlying bi-party contract will be for a contribution of any type, the work content or objective of which is sufficiently defined to permit a conventional NEC contract to be signed.

Parties must recognise that by entering into a contract with the TSSC multi-party partnering clause they will be undertaking responsibilities additional to those in the basic NEC contract.

A dispute (or difference) between Partners who do not have a contract between themselves is resolved by the Core Group. This is the Group that manages the conduct of the Partners in accordance with the Partnering Information. If the Core Group is unable to resolve the issue, then it is resolved under the procedure of the Partners' Own Contracts, either directly or indirectly with the *Client,* who will always be involved at some stage in the contractual chain. The *Client* may seek to have the issues on all contracts dealt with simultaneously.

The TSSC multi-party partnering clause does not include direct remedies between non-contracting Partners to recover losses suffered by one of them caused by a failure of the other. These remedies remain available in each Partner's Own Contract, but their existence will encourage the parties to compromise any differences that arise.

This applies at all levels of the supply chain, as a *Contractor who* is a Partner retains the responsibility for actions of a subcontractor who is a Partner.

The final sanction against any Partner who fails to act as stated in the TSSC multi-party partnering clause is for the Partner who employed them not to invite them to partner again.

TSSC multi-party partnering

The TSSC multi-party partnering clause is incorporated into the Own Contract of a Partner as follows.

1. The additional conditions below (referred to as Z1 but should be numbered to suit) would be inserted in the 'additional conditions' provision in the Contract Data.

2. Add the following entry to the Contract Data in each bi-party contract:

- The *Client* is

  Name. . . . .

  Address . . . .

  . . . .

- The *Client*'s *objective* is . . . .

  . . . .

  . . . .

  . . . .

  . . . .

  . . . .

  . . . .

- The Partnering Information is in

  . . . .

  . . . .

  . . . .

  . . . .

TSSC multi-party partnering

Z1: Partnering

Identified and defined terms   Z1.1

(1) The Partners are those named in the Schedule of Partners. The *Client* is a Partner.

(2) An Own Contract is a contract between two Partners which includes this clause.

(3) The Core Group comprises the Partners listed in the Schedule of Core Group Members.

(4) Partnering Information is information which specifies how the Partners work together and is either in the documents which the Contract Data states it is in or in an instruction given in accordance with this contract.

(5) A Key Performance Indicator is an aspect of performance for which a target is stated in the Schedule of Partners.

Actions   Z1.2

(1) Each Partner works with the other Partners to achieve the *Client*'s *objective* stated in the Contract Data and the objectives of every other Partner stated in the Schedule of Partners.

(2) Each Partner nominates a representative to act for it in dealings with other Partners.

(3) The Core Group acts and takes decisions on behalf of the Partners on those matters stated in the Partnering Information.

(4) The Partners select the members of the Core Group. The Core Group decides how they will work and decides the dates when each member joins and leaves the Core Group. The *Client*'s representative leads the Core Group unless stated otherwise in the Partnering Information.

(5) The Core Group keeps the Schedule of Core Group Members and the Schedule of Partners up to date and issues copies of them to the Partners each time either is revised.

(6) This clause does not create a legal partnership between Partners who are not one of the Parties in this contract.

Working together   Z1.3

(1) The Partners work together as stated in the Partnering Information and in a spirit of mutual trust and co-operation.

(2) A Partner may ask another Partner to provide information which he needs to carry out the work in his Own Contract and the other Partner provides it.

(3) Each Partner gives an early warning to the other Partners when he becomes aware of any matter that could affect the achievement of another Partner's objectives stated in the Schedule of Partners.

(4) The Partners use common information systems as set out in the Partnering Information.

(5) A Partner implements a decision of the Core Group by issuing instructions in accordance with its Own Contracts.

(6) The Core Group may give an instruction to the Partners to change the Partnering Information. Each such change to the Partnering Information is a compensation event which may lead to reduced Prices.

(7) The Core Group prepares and maintains a timetable showing the proposed timing of the contributions of the Partners. The Core Group issues a copy of the timetable to the Partners each time it is revised. The *Contractor* changes his programme if it is necessary to do so in order to comply with the revised timetable. Each such change is a compensation event which may lead to reduced Prices.

(8) A Partner gives advice, information and opinion to the Core Group and to other Partners when asked to do so by the Core Group. This advice, information and opinion relates to work that another Partner is carrying out under its Own Contract and is given fully, openly and objectively. The Partners show contingency and risk allowances in information about costs, prices and timing for future work.

(9) A Partner notifies the Core Group before subcontracting any work.

Incentives Z1.4 (1) A Partner is paid the amount stated in the Schedule of Partners if the target stated for a Key Performance Indicator is improved upon or achieved. Payment of the amount is due when the target has been improved upon or achieved and is made as part of the amount due in the Partner's Own Contract.

(2) The *Client* may add a Key Performance Indicator and associated payment to the Schedule of Partners but may not delete or reduce a payment stated in the Schedule of Partners.

Guidance notes on TSSC multi-party partnering clauses

Identified and defined terms

Clause Z1.2 (1)
The point at which someone becomes a Partner is when his Own Contract (which includes the TSSC multi-party partnering clause) comes into existence. They should then be named in the Schedule of Partners, and their representative identified.

Clause Z1.2 (3)
Not every Partner is a member of the Core Group.

Clause Z1.2 (5)
There are two options for subcontractor partners. Either the amount payable cascades down if the schedule allocates the same bonus/cost to the main contractor and subcontractor, or the main contractor absorbs the bonus/cost and does not pass it on.

Working together

Clause Z1.3 (5)
The Core Group organises and holds meetings. It produces and distributes records of each meeting which include agreed actions. Instructions from the Core Group are issued in accordance with the Partner's Own Contract. The Core Group may invite other Partners or people to a meeting of the Core Group.

Clause Z1.3 (8)
The Partners should give advice and assistance when asked, and in addition whenever they identify something that would be helpful to another Partner.

Clause Z1.3 (9)
A subcontractor/subconsultant may be a Partner, but the general policy on this should be decided at the beginning of the Project. The Core Group should advise the Contractor/Consultant at the outset if a subcontractor/subconsultant is to be asked to be a Partner. A subcontractor/subconsultant who the Core group decides should be a Partner should not be appointed if he is unwilling to be a Partner.

Possible alternative incentive KPI

Incentives

Clause Z1.4 (1) (also 'Z1.1 (1) and Z1.3 (3)')
If one Partner lets the others down for a particular target by poor performance, then all lose their bonus for that target. If the *Employer* tries to prevent a target being met, he is in breach of clause 10.1.

There can be more than one KPI for each partner. KPIs may apply to one Partner, to several partners or to all partners.

An example of a KPI

KPI	Number of days to complete each floor of the building framework
Target	14 days
Measurement	Number of days between removal of falsework from the entire slab and from the slab below
Amount	Main contractor – £5,000 each floor Formwork and concrete sub-contractor – £2,000 each floor Structural designer – £750 each floor

Clause Z1.4 (2)
The *Client* should consult with the other Partners before adding a KPI. The effect on subcontracted work should be noted; adding a KPI to work which is subcontracted can involve a change to the KPI for a subcontractor/subconsultant.

Incentives

KPI ability of *Contractor* to complete repair works correctly first time - only applied to *Contractor*

Target	5%
Measurement	Number of recalls arising from defective or incomplete work expressed as a percentage of the number of repairs completed
Amount	0.05% of relevant component of PSPD for repairs

Flow charts for the

Term Service Short Contract

FLOW CHARTS

PREFACE

These flow charts depict the procedures followed when using the NEC3 Term Service Short Contract (TSSC). They are intended to help people using the TSSC to see how the various TSSC clauses produce clear and precise sequences of action for the people involved.

The flow charts are not part of any contract. Much of the text and many of the words taken from the TSSC itself are abbreviated in the flow charts. The flow charts depict almost all of the sequences of action set out in the TSSC. Many of the sequences interact, and because of this, users of the flow charts will often have to review more than one sheet in order to track the full sequence of actions in one area.

ABBREVIATIONS USED IN THE FLOW CHART BOXES

FC 16	Flow chart for clause 16
E	*Employer*
C	*Contractor*
SC	Subcontractor
CD	Contract Data
CE	Compensation event
SI	Service Information

                                         www.neccontract.com

Legend

CHART START

HEADINGS
    Headings in caps
    provide guidance

STATEMENTS
    If a clause is
    referenced, text
    is from the NEC

LOGIC LINKS
    Links go to right
    and/or downward
    unless shown

QUESTION
    Answer question
    to determine the
    route to follow

SUBROUTINE
    Include another
    flow chart here

CONTINUATION
    Link to matching
    point(s) on other
    chart sheets

CHART TITLE
    Chart number,
    title and sheet

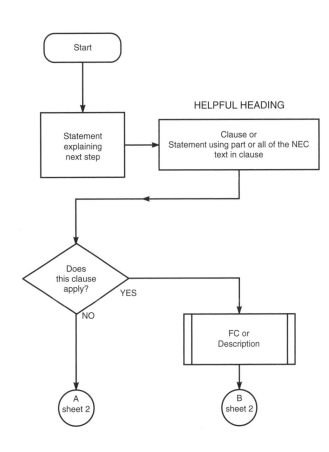

**Flow chart or Sheet 1 of 2
Description**

CONTINUATION

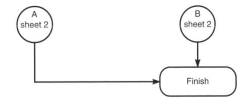

CHART FINISH

**Flow chart or Sheet 2 of 2
Description**

CHART TITLE

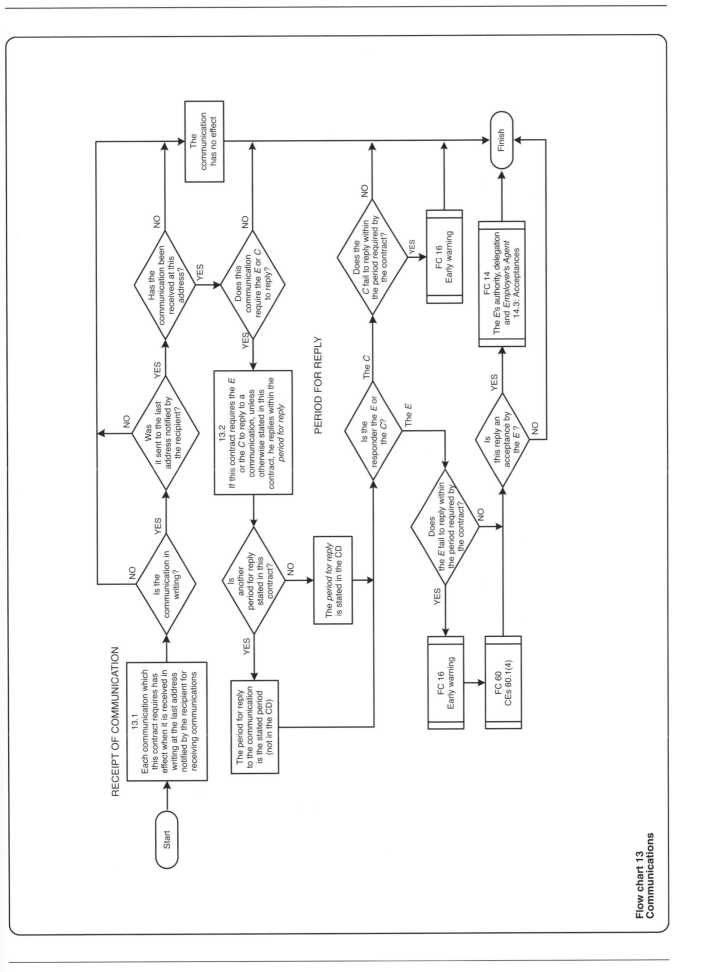

RECEIPT OF COMMUNICATION

Start

13.1
Each communication which this contract requires has effect when it is received in writing at the last address notified by the recipient for receiving communications

Is the communication in writing? — NO → Was it sent to the last address notified by the recipient? — NO → The communication has no effect

YES

Was it sent to the last address notified by the recipient? — YES → Has the communication been received at this address? — NO → The communication has no effect

Has the communication been received at this address? — YES

Does this communication require the E or C to reply? — NO → The communication has no effect

Does this communication require the E or C to reply? — YES

13.2
If this contract requires the E or the C to reply to a communication, unless otherwise stated in this contract, he replies within the *period for reply*

Is another period for reply stated in this contract? — YES → The period for reply to the communication is the stated period (not in the CD)

Is another period for reply stated in this contract? — NO → The *period for reply* is stated in the CD

PERIOD FOR REPLY

Is the responder the E or the C? — The C → Does the C fail to reply within the period required by the contract? — NO → Finish

Does the C fail to reply within the period required by the contract? — YES → FC 16 Early warning

Is the responder the E or the C? — The E → Does the E fail to reply within the period required by the contract? — NO → Is this reply an acceptance by the E? — YES → FC 14 The E's authority, delegation and *Employer's Agent* 14.3: Acceptances → Finish

Is this reply an acceptance by the E? — NO → Finish

Does the E fail to reply within the period required by the contract? — YES → FC 16 Early warning → FC 60 CEs 60.1(4)

Flow chart 13
Communications

Start

Does the E wish to instruct a Task?
- YES → **A Sheet 2**
- NO

B Sheet 2 →

EMPLOYER INSTRUCTION

14.1
The C obeys an instruction which is in accordance with this contract and is given to him by the E

FC 13 Communications

CHANGING SERVICE INFORMATION

14.2
The E may give an instruction to the C which changes the SI or a Task Order

11.2(6)
SI is information which either
- specifies and describes the service or states any constraints on how the C Provides the Service

and is either
- in the document called "SI" or
- in an instruction given in accordance with this contract

11.2(5)
To Provide the Service means to do the work necessary to provide the service in accordance with this contract and all incidental work, services and actions which this contract requires

The service is stated in the CD

Is this an instruction to make a Defect acceptable?
- NO
- YES

FC 60 Compensation events 60.1(1)

THE CONTRACTOR'S RESPONSIBILITY

14.3
The E's acceptance of a communication from the C or of his work does not change the C's responsibility to Provide the Service

DELEGATION

14.4
The E, after notifying the C, may delegate any of the E's actions and may cancel any delegation. A reference to an action of the E in this contract includes an action by his delegate

C Sheet 4

Flow chart 14 Sheet 1 of 4
The Employer's authority, delegation and Employer's Agent

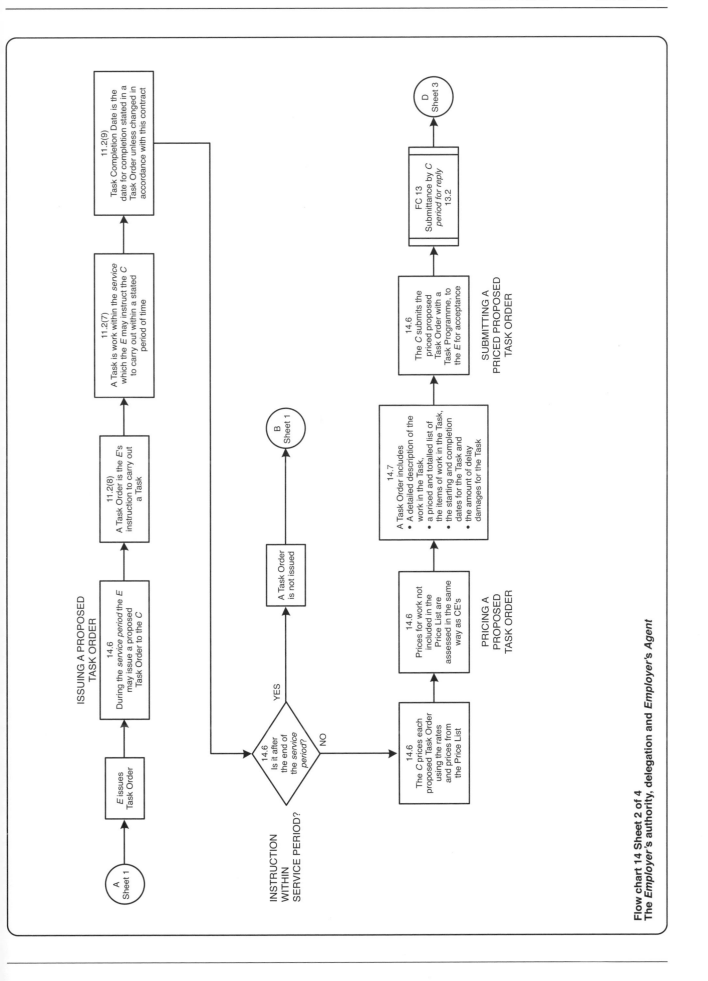

ISSUING A PROPOSED TASK ORDER

A
Sheet 1

E issues
Task Order

14.6
During the *service period* the *E*
may issue a proposed
Task Order to the *C*

11.2(8)
A Task Order is the *E*'s
instruction to carry out
a Task

11.2(7)
A Task is work within the *service*
which the *E* may instruct the *C*
to carry out within a stated
period of time

11.2(9)
Task Completion Date is the
date for completion stated in a
Task Order unless changed in
accordance with this contract

**INSTRUCTION
WITHIN
SERVICE PERIOD?**

14.6
Is it after
the end of
the *service
period?*

YES

B
Sheet 1

A Task Order
is not issued

NO

14.6
The *C* prices each
proposed Task Order
using the rates
and prices from
the Price List

14.6
Prices for work not
included in the
Price List are
assessed in the same
way as CE's

**PRICING A
PROPOSED
TASK ORDER**

14.7
A Task Order includes
• A detailed description of the
  work in the Task,
• a priced and totalled list of
  the items of work in the Task,
• the starting and completion
  dates for the Task and
• the amount of delay
  damages for the Task

14.6
The *C* submits the
priced proposed
Task Order with a
Task Programme, to
the *E* for acceptance

**SUBMITTING A
PRICED PROPOSED
TASK ORDER**

FC 13
Submittance by *C*
period for reply
13.2

D
Sheet 3

Flow chart 14 Sheet 2 of 4
The *Employer's* authority, delegation and *Employer's Agent*

Flow chart 14 Sheet 3 of 4
The *Employer's* authority, delegation and *Employer's Agent*

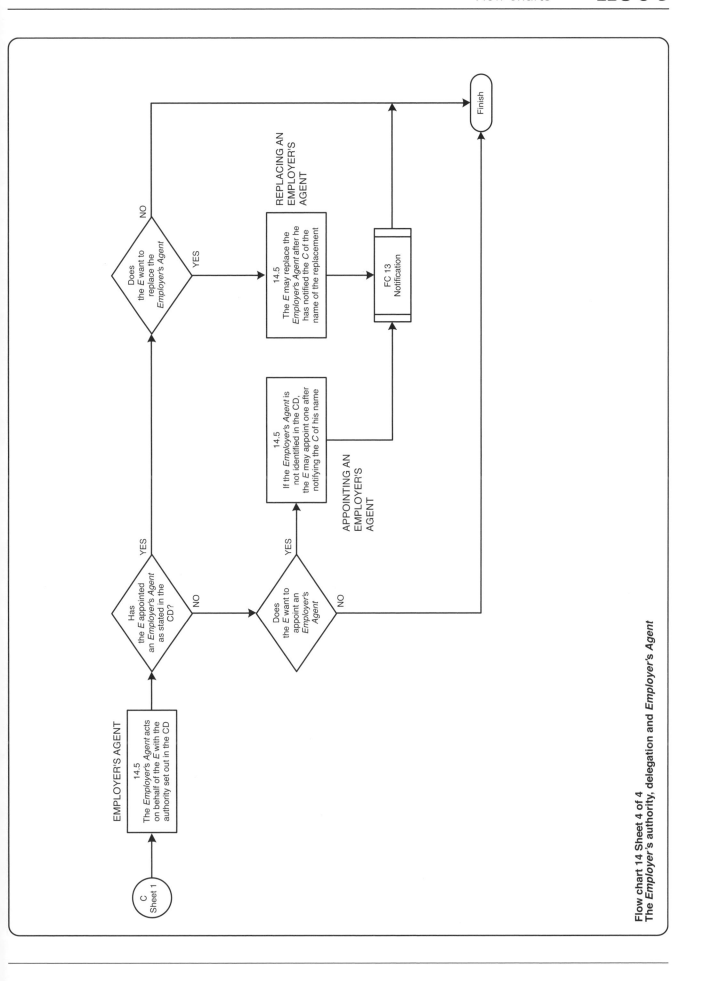

Flow chart 14 Sheet 4 of 4
The *Employer's* authority, delegation and *Employer's Agent*

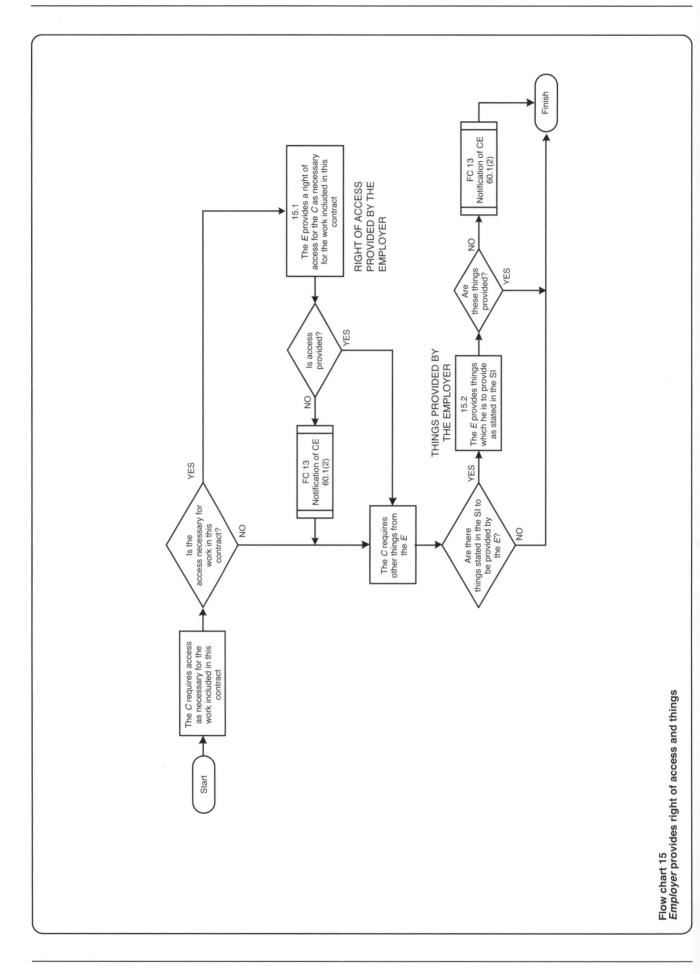

Start

The *C* requires access as necessary for the work included in this contract

Is the access necessary for work in this contract?

NO → FC 13 Notification of CE 60.1(2)

YES →

15.1
The *E* provides a right of access for the *C* as necessary for the work included in this contract

RIGHT OF ACCESS PROVIDED BY THE EMPLOYER

Is access provided?

NO → FC 13 Notification of CE 60.1(2)

YES →

The *C* requires other things from the *E*

Are there things stated in the SI to be provided by the *E*?

YES →

15.2
The *E* provides things which he is to provide as stated in the SI

THINGS PROVIDED BY THE EMPLOYER

NO →

Are these things provided?

NO → FC 13 Notification of CE 60.1(2) → **Finish**

YES →

Flow chart 15
Employer **provides right of access and things**

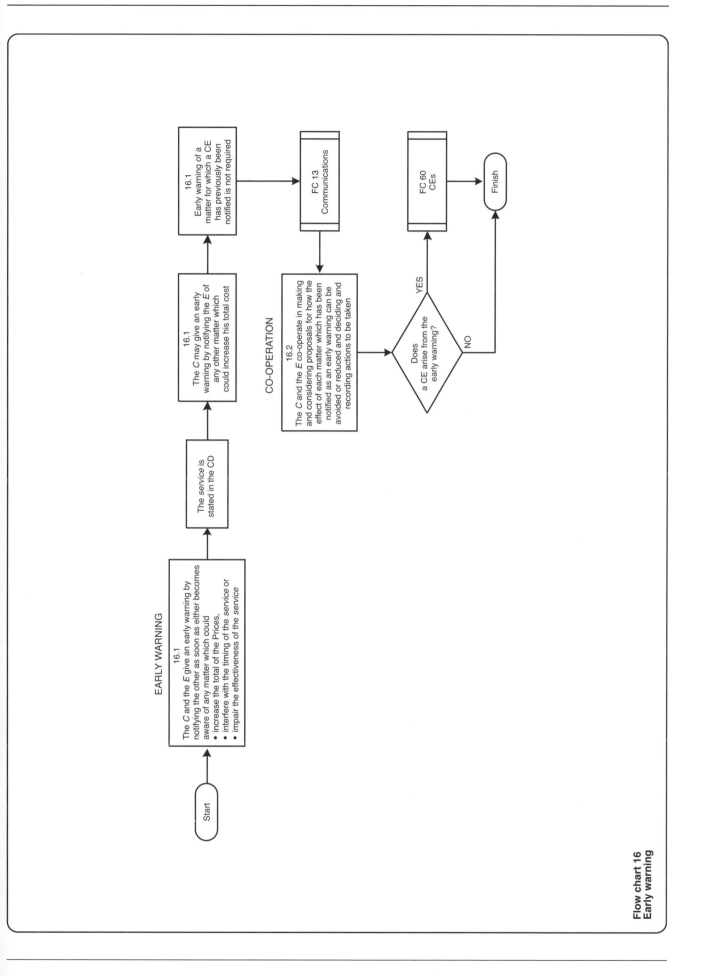

EARLY WARNING

Start

16.1
The *C* and the *E* give an early warning by notifying the other as soon as either becomes aware of any matter which could
- increase the total of the Prices,
- interfere with the timing of the *service* or
- impair the effectiveness of the *service*

The *service* is stated in the CD

16.1
The *C* may give an early warning by notifying the *E* of any other matter which could increase his total cost

16.1
Early warning of a matter for which a CE has previously been notified is not required

CO-OPERATION

16.2
The *C* and the *E* co-operate in making and considering proposals for how the effect of each matter which has been notified as an early warning can be avoided or reduced and deciding and recording actions to be taken

FC 13
Communications

Does a CE arise from the early warning?

YES

NO

FC 60
CEs

Finish

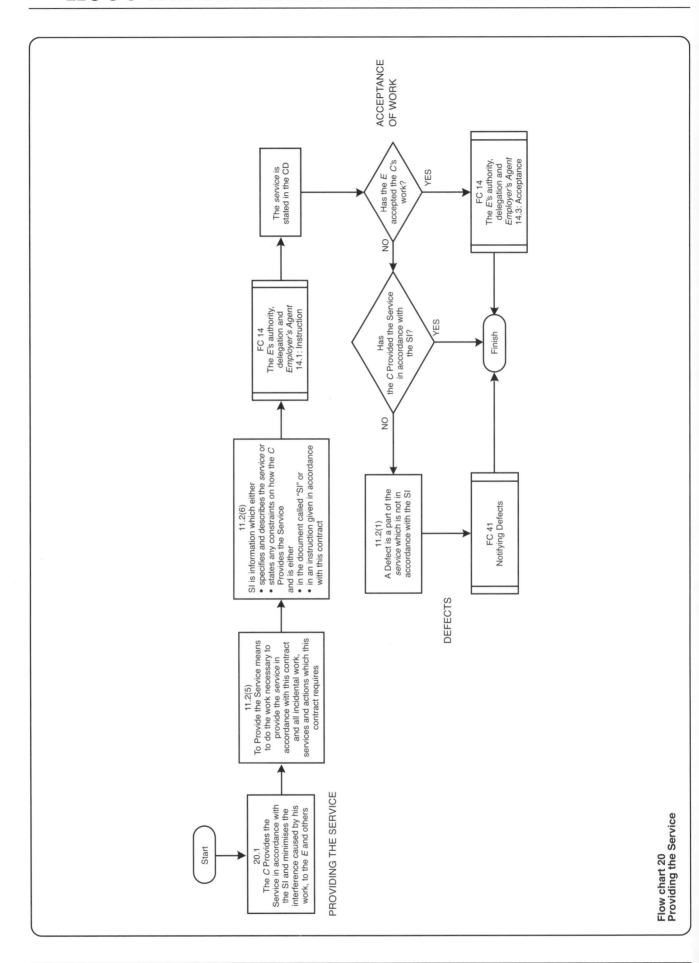

ACCEPTANCE OF WORK

The service is stated in the CD

FC 14
The *E's* authority, delegation and *Employer's Agent*
14.1: Instruction

Has the *E* accepted the *C's* work?

NO

YES

FC 14
The *E's* authority, delegation and *Employer's Agent*
14.3: Acceptance

Has the *C* Provided the Service in accordance with the SI?

YES

NO

Finish

11.2(6)
SI is information which either
• specifies and describes the *service* or
• states any constraints on how the *C* Provides the Service
and is either
• in the document called "SI" or
• in an instruction given in accordance with this contract

11.2(1)
A Defect is a part of the *service* which is not in accordance with the SI

FC 41
Notifying Defects

DEFECTS

Start

20.1
The *C* Provides the Service in accordance with the SI and minimises the interference caused by his work, to the *E* and others

11.2(5)
To Provide the Service means to do the work necessary to provide the *service* in accordance with this contract and all incidental work, services and actions which this contract requires

PROVIDING THE SERVICE

Flow chart 20
Providing the Service

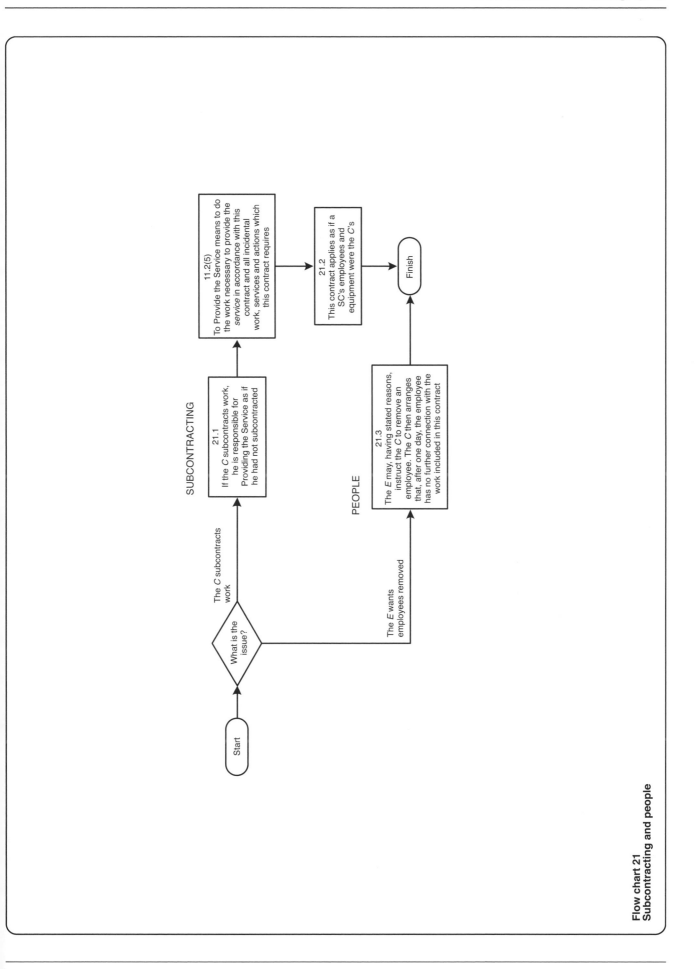

Flow chart 21
Subcontracting and people

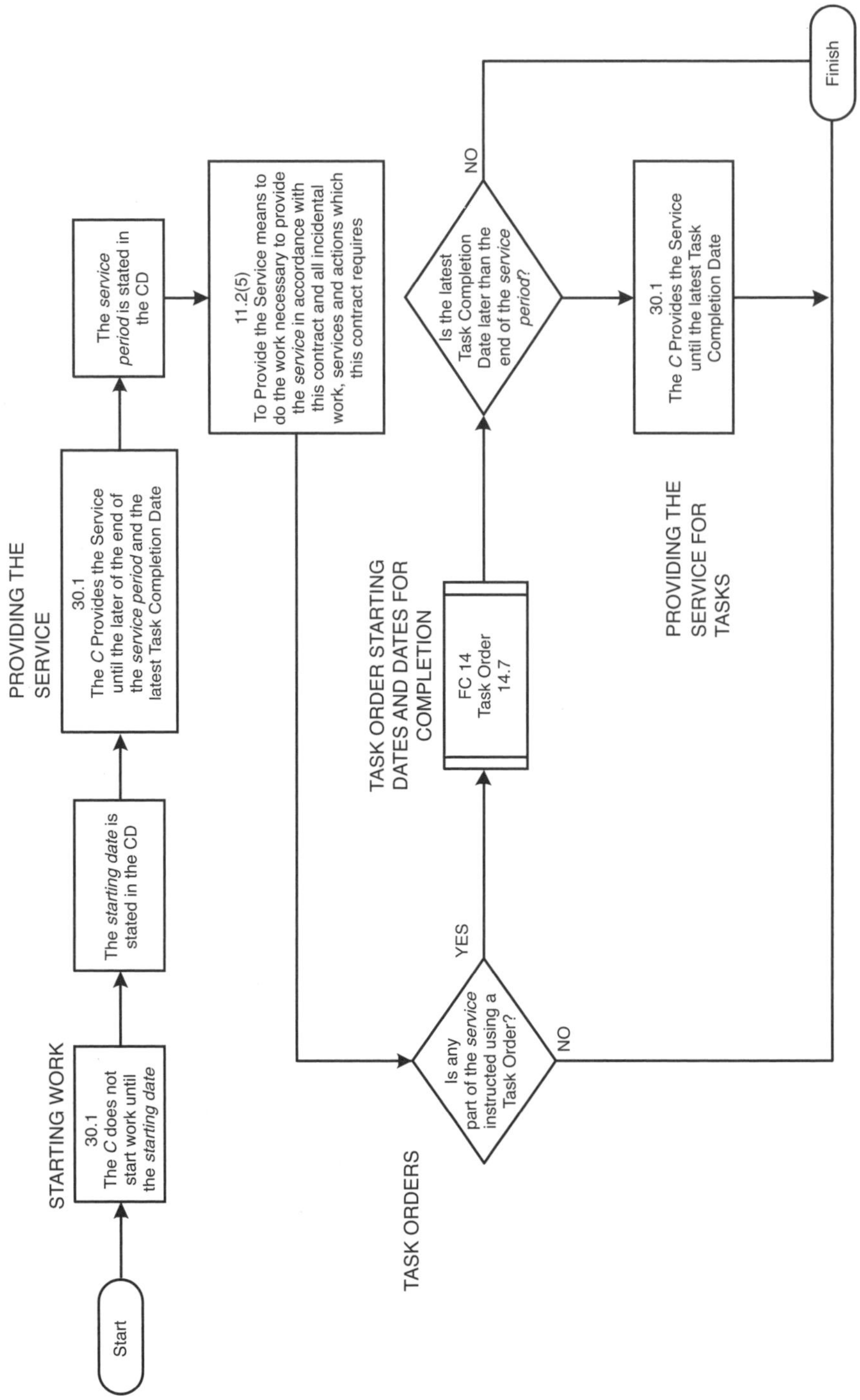

STARTING WORK

Start

30.1
The C does not start work until the *starting date*

The *starting date* is stated in the CD

PROVIDING THE SERVICE

30.1
The C Provides the Service until the later of the end of the *service period* and the latest Task Completion Date

The *service period* is stated in the CD

11.2(5)
To Provide the Service means to do the work necessary to provide the *service* in accordance with this contract and all incidental work, services and actions which this contract requires

TASK ORDERS

Is any part of the *service* instructed using a Task Order?

YES

TASK ORDER STARTING DATES AND DATES FOR COMPLETION

FC 14
Task Order
14.7

Is the latest Task Completion Date later than the end of the *service period?*

NO → Finish

YES ↑

NO

PROVIDING THE SERVICE FOR TASKS

30.1
The C Provides the Service until the latest Task Completion Date

Flow chart 30
Starting and the *service period*

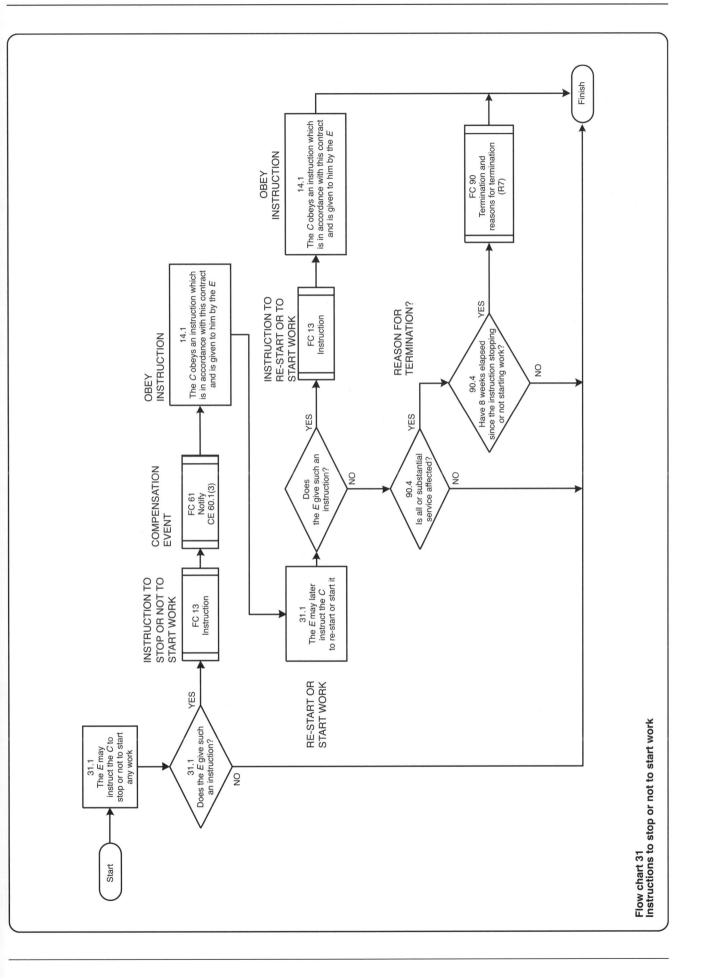

Flow chart 31
Instructions to stop or not to start work

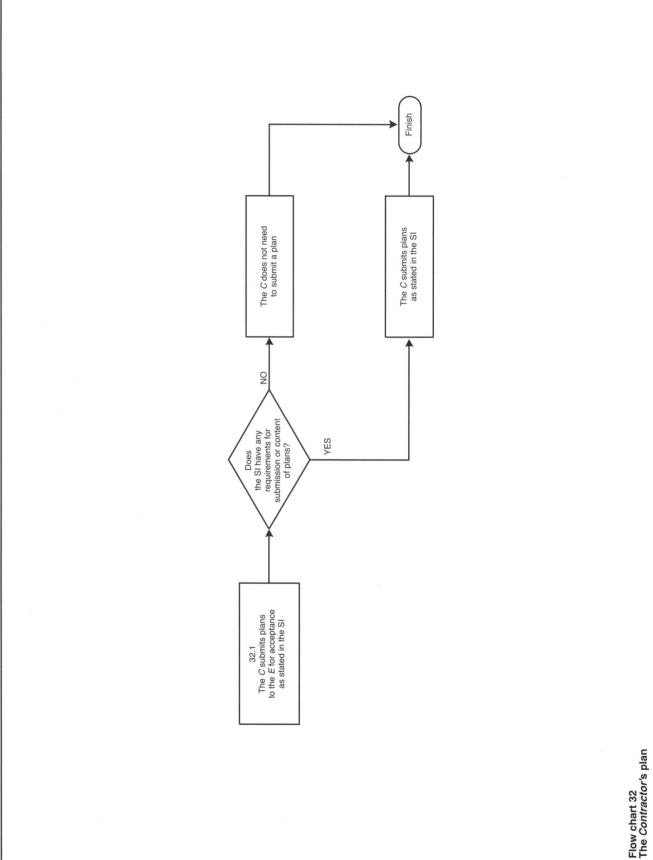

Flow chart 32
The *Contractor*'s plan

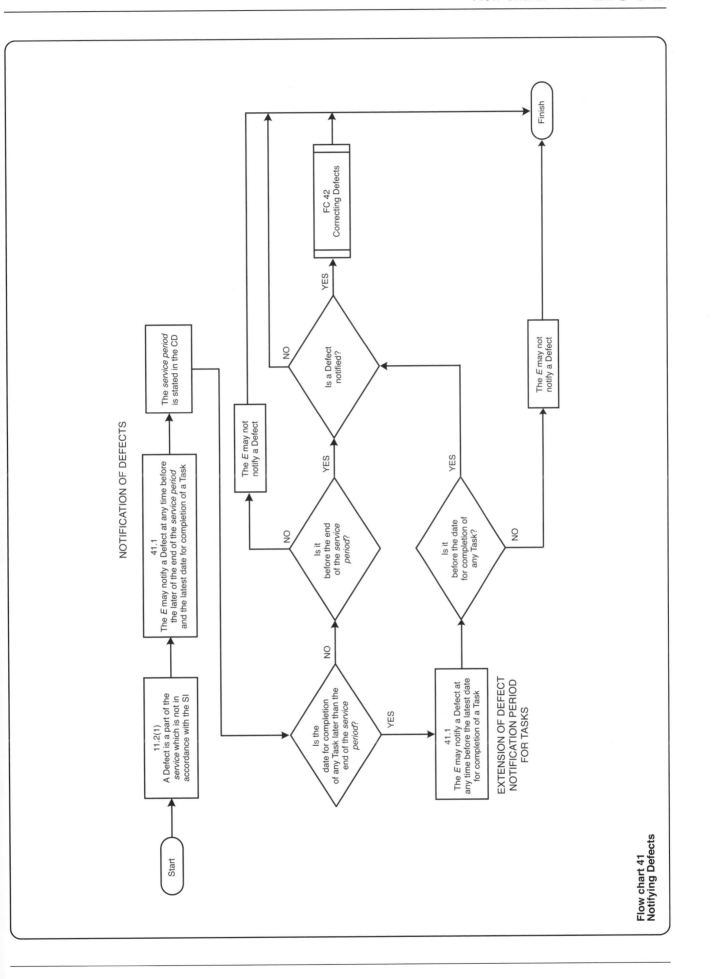

NOTIFICATION OF DEFECTS

Start

11.2(1)
A Defect is a part of the *service* which is not in accordance with the SI

41.1
The *E* may notify a Defect at any time before the later of the end of the *service period* and the latest date for completion of a Task

The *service period* is stated in the CD

Is the date for completion of any Task later than the end of the *service period?*

NO → Is it before the end of the *service period?*

YES → Is a Defect notified?

The *E* may not notify a Defect

YES → FC 42 Correcting Defects

NO → The *E* may not notify a Defect

YES (from "Is the date for completion...") →
41.1
The *E* may notify a Defect at any time before the latest date for completion of a Task

EXTENSION OF DEFECT NOTIFICATION PERIOD FOR TASKS

Is it before the date for completion of any Task?

YES → (up to "Is a Defect notified?")

NO → The *E* may not notify a Defect

Finish

Flow chart 41
Notifying Defects

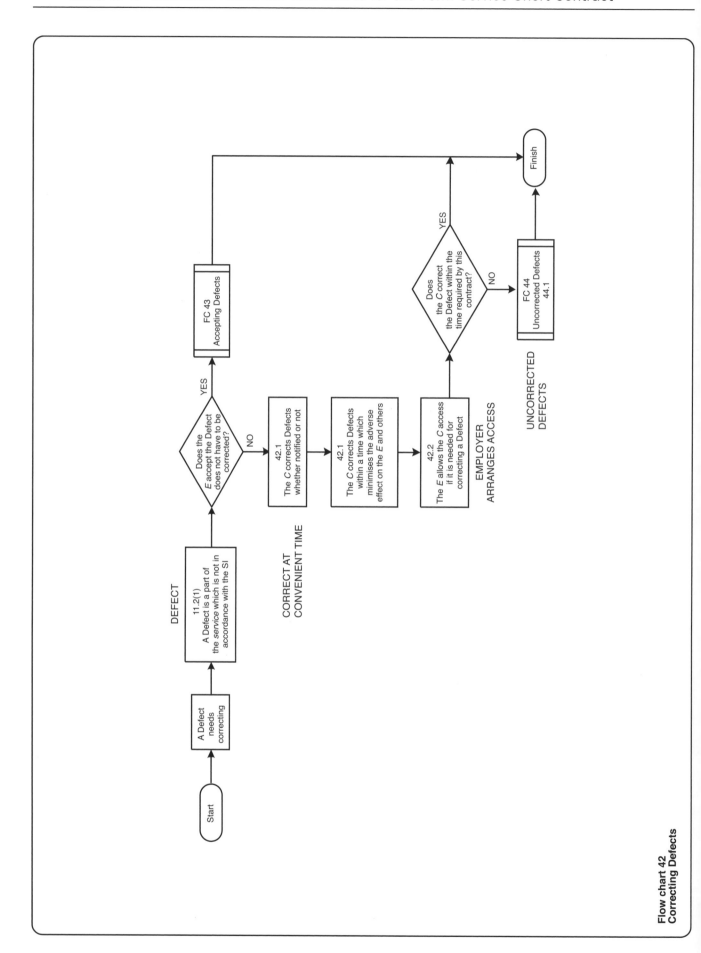

**Flow chart 42
Correcting Defects**

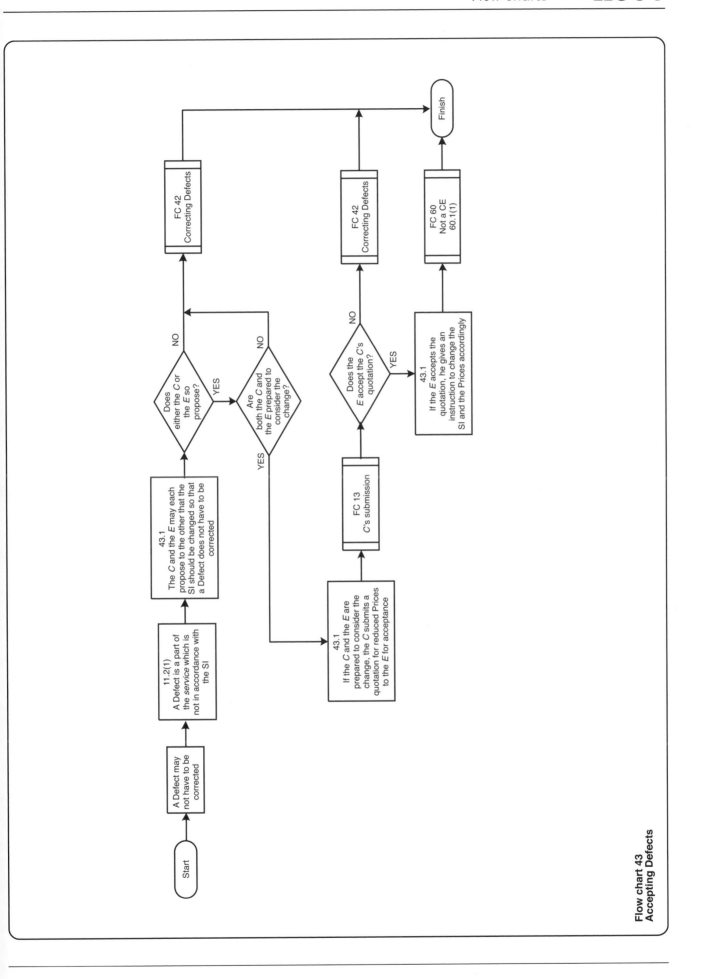

Start

A Defect may not have to be corrected

11.2(1)
A Defect is a part of the *service* which is not in accordance with the SI

43.1
The *C* and the *E* may each propose to the other that the SI should be changed so that a Defect does not have to be corrected

Does either the *C* or the *E* so propose?

NO → FC 42 Correcting Defects

YES

Are both the *C* and the *E* prepared to consider the change?

NO → (to FC 42 Correcting Defects)

YES

43.1
If the *C* and the *E* are prepared to consider the change, the *C* submits a quotation for reduced Prices to the *E* for acceptance

FC 13
C's submission

Does the *E* accept the *C*'s quotation?

NO → FC 42 Correcting Defects

YES

43.1
If the *E* accepts the quotation, he gives an instruction to change the SI and the Prices accordingly

FC 60
Not a CE
60.1(1)

Finish

Flow chart 43
Accepting Defects

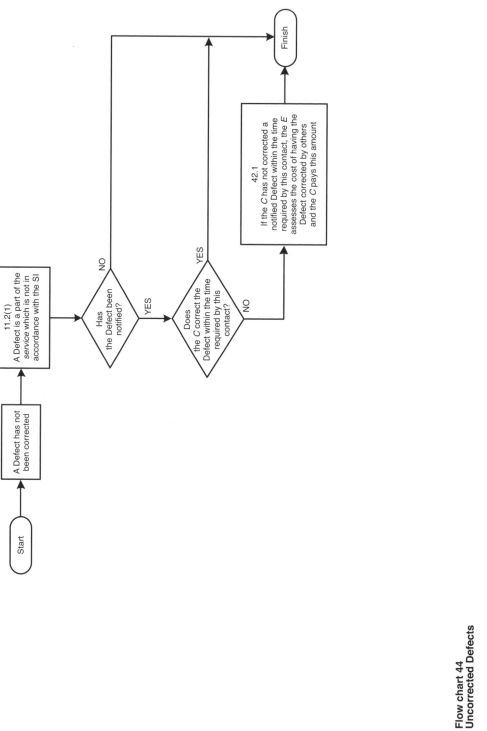

Flow chart 44
Uncorrected Defects

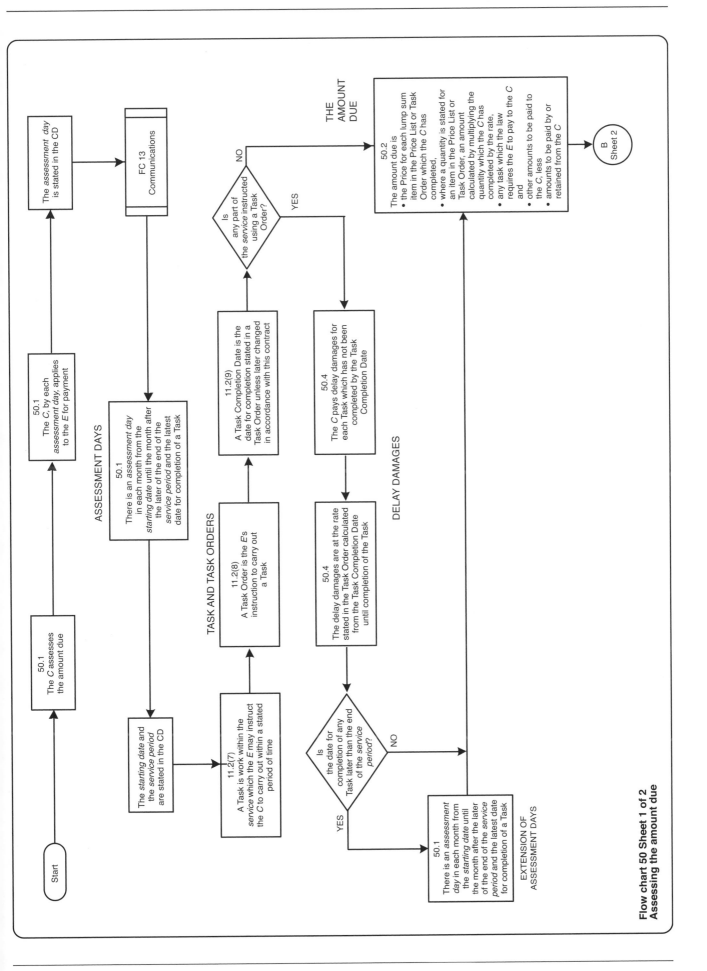

THE
AMOUNT
DUE

50.2
The amount due is
• the Price for each lump sum
  item in the Price List or Task
  Order which the C has
  completed,
• where a quantity is stated for
  an item in the Price List or
  Task Order, an amount
  calculated by multiplying the
  quantity which the C has
  completed by the rate,
• any task which the law
  requires the E to pay to the C
and
• other amounts to be paid to
  the C, less
• amounts to be paid by or
  retained from the C

B
Sheet 2

The *assessment day*
is stated in the CD

FC 13
Communications

NO

Is
any part of
the *service* instructed
using a Task
Order?

YES

50.1
The C, by each
assessment day, applies
to the E for payment

ASSESSMENT DAYS

50.1
There is an *assessment day*
in each month from the
starting date until the month after
the later of the end of the
service period and the latest
date for completion of a Task

11.2(9)
A Task Completion Date is the
date for completion stated in a
Task Order unless later changed
in accordance with this contract

50.4
The C pays delay damages for
each Task which has not been
completed by the Task
Completion Date

50.1
The C assesses
the amount due

TASK AND TASK ORDERS

11.2(8)
A Task Order is the E's
instruction to carry out
a Task

50.4
The delay damages are at the rate
stated in the Task Order calculated
from the Task Completion Date
until completion of the Task

DELAY DAMAGES

50.1
The *starting date* and
the *service period*
are stated in the CD

11.2(7)
A Task is work within the
service which the E may instruct
the C to carry out within a stated
period of time

Is
the date for
completion of any
Task later than the end
of the *service
period*?

NO

YES

Start

50.1
There is an *assessment
day* in each month from
the *starting date* until
the month after the later
of the end of the *service
period* and the latest date
for completion of a Task

EXTENSION OF
ASSESSMENT DAYS

**Flow chart 50 Sheet 1 of 2
Assessing the amount due**

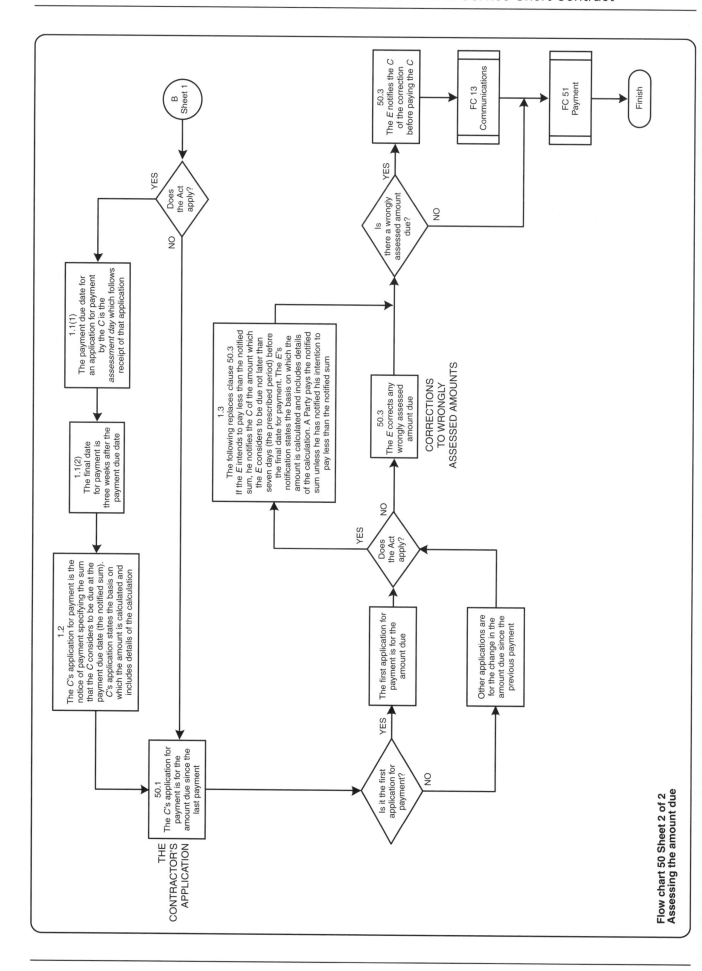

Flow chart 50 Sheet 2 of 2
Assessing the amount due

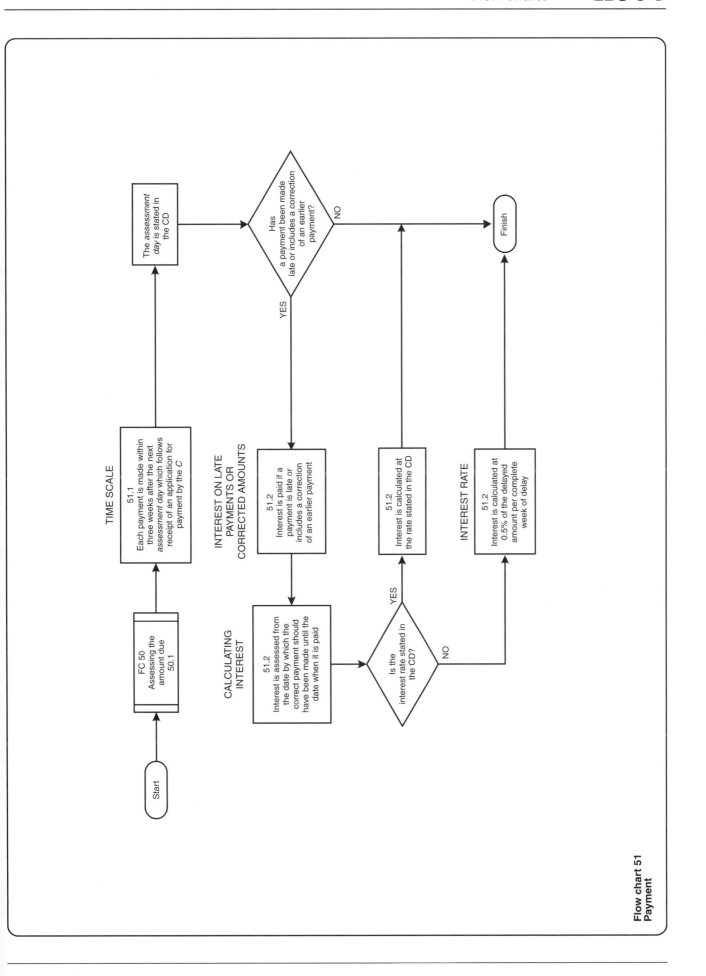

TIME SCALE

FC 50
Assessing the
amount due
50.1

Start

51.1
Each payment is made within
three weeks after the next
assessment day which follows
receipt of an application for
payment by the *C*

The *assessment
day* is stated in
the CD

Has
a payment been made
late or includes a correction
of an earlier
payment?

YES

NO

INTEREST ON LATE
PAYMENTS OR
CORRECTED AMOUNTS

51.2
Interest is paid if a
payment is late or
includes a correction
of an earlier payment

CALCULATING
INTEREST

51.2
Interest is assessed from
the date by which the
correct payment should
have been made until the
date when it is paid

Is the
interest rate stated in
the CD?

YES

NO

51.2
Interest is calculated at
the rate stated in the CD

INTEREST RATE

51.2
Interest is calculated at
0.5% of the delayed
amount per complete
week of delay

Finish

Flow chart 51
Payment

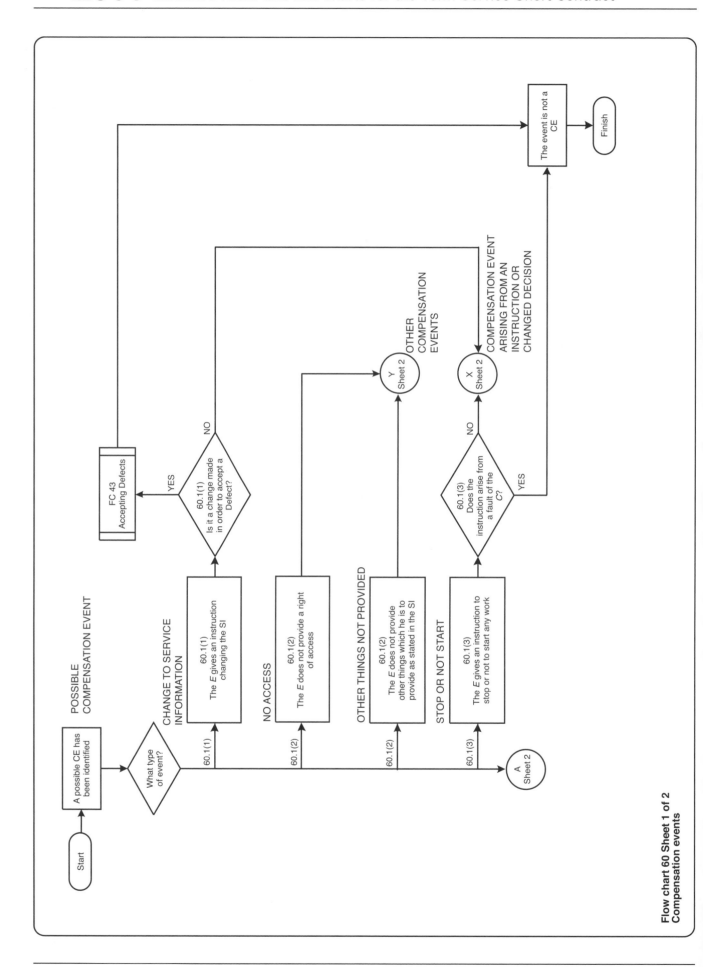

Flow chart 60 Sheet 1 of 2
Compensation events

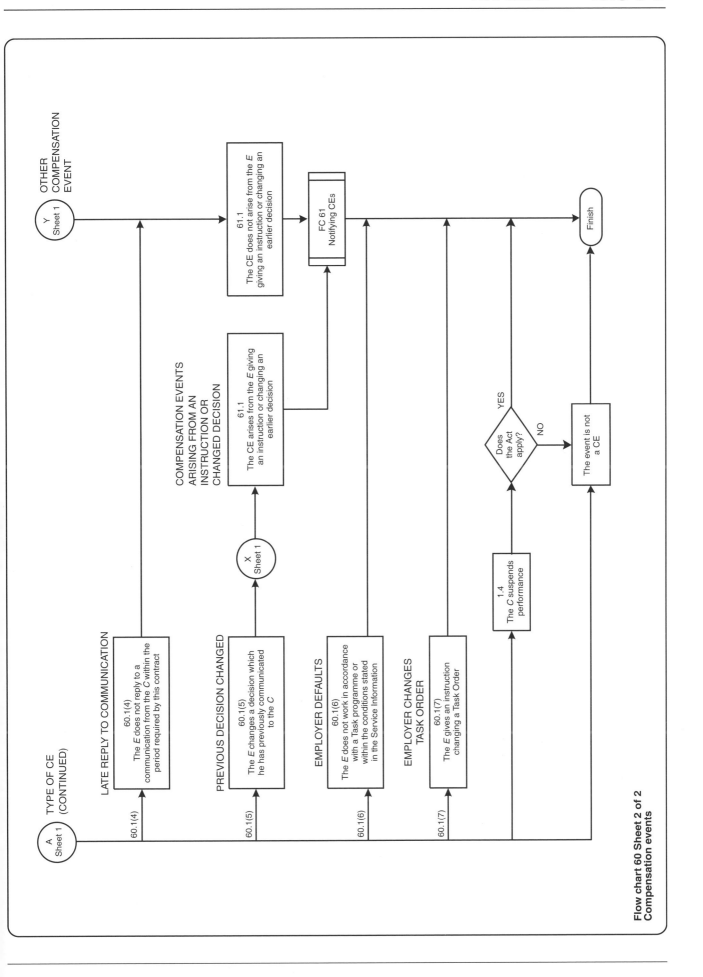

Flow chart 60 Sheet 2 of 2
Compensation events

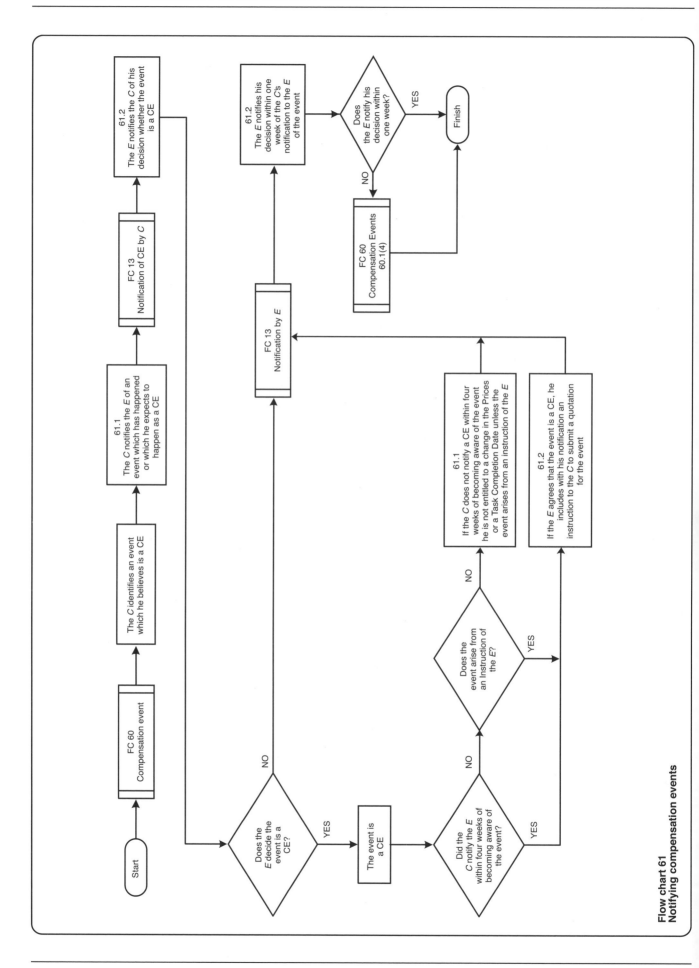

Flow chart 61
Notifying compensation events

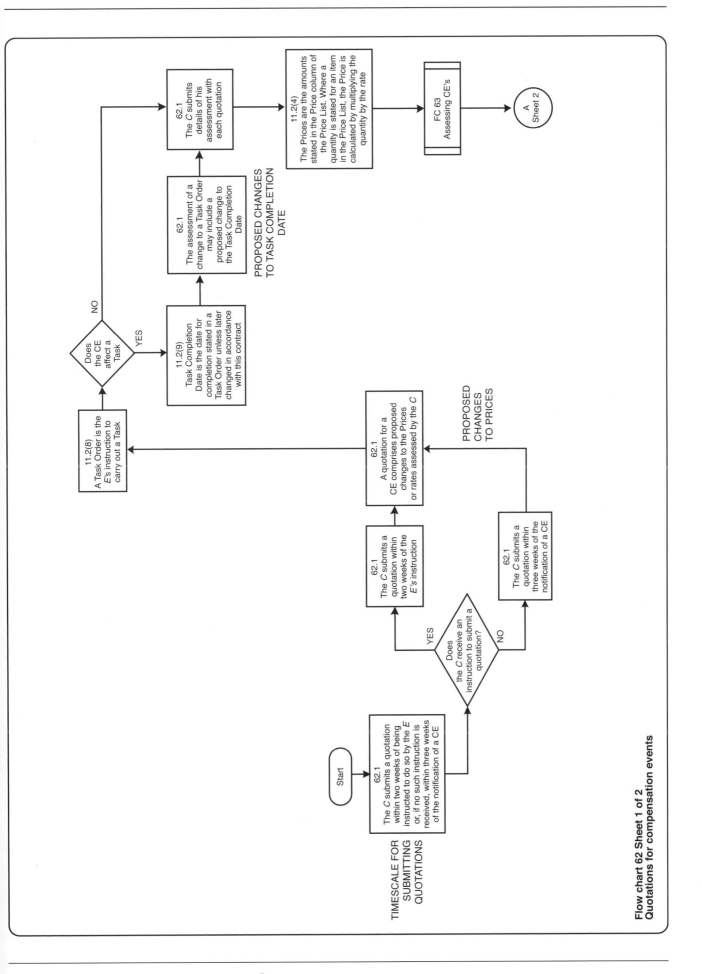

62.1
The *C* submits details of his assessment with each quotation

11.2(4)
The Prices are the amounts stated in the Price column of the Price List. Where a quantity is stated for an item in the Price List, the Price is calculated by multiplying the quantity by the rate

FC 63
Assessing CE's

A
Sheet 2

62.1
The assessment of a change to a Task Order may include a proposed change to the Task Completion Date

PROPOSED CHANGES
TO TASK COMPLETION
DATE

NO

Does the CE affect a Task

YES

11.2(9)
Task Completion Date is the date for completion stated in a Task Order unless later changed in accordance with this contract

11.2(8)
A Task Order is the *E*'s instruction to carry out a Task

62.1
A quotation for a CE comprises proposed changes to the Prices or rates assessed by the *C*

PROPOSED
CHANGES
TO PRICES

62.1
The *C* submits a quotation within two weeks of the *E*'s instruction

62.1
The *C* submits a quotation within three weeks of the notification of a CE

YES

Does the *C* receive an instruction to submit a quotation?

NO

Start

62.1
The *C* submits a quotation within two weeks of being instructed to do so by the *E* or, if no such instruction is received, within three weeks of the notification of a CE

TIMESCALE FOR
SUBMITTING
QUOTATIONS

Flow chart 62 Sheet 1 of 2
Quotations for compensation events

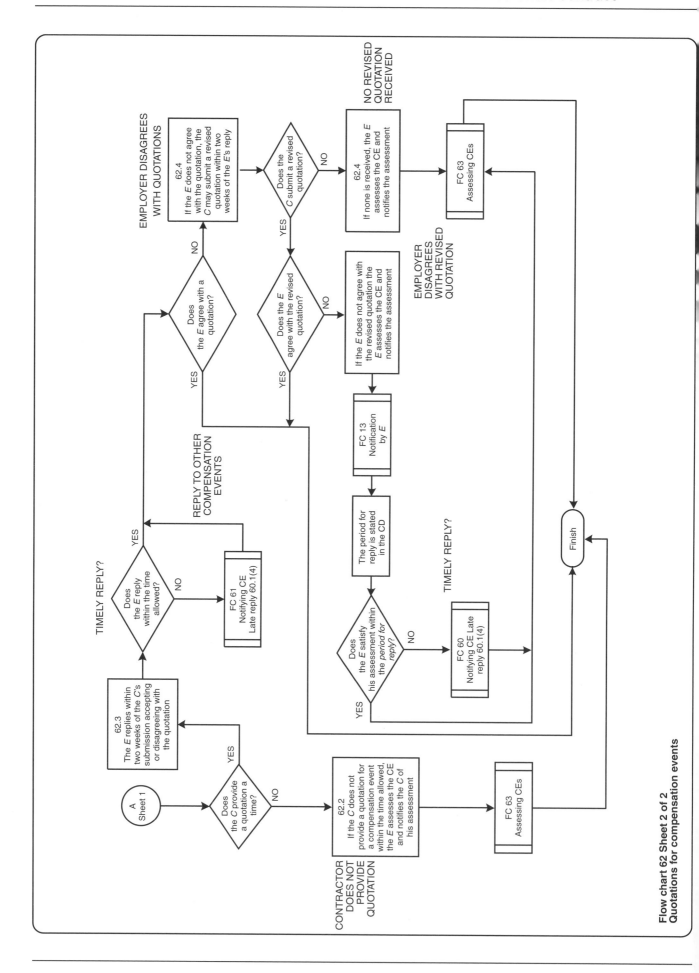

EMPLOYER DISAGREES WITH QUOTATIONS

62.4 If the *E* does not agree with the quotation, the *C* may submit a revised quotation within two weeks of the *E*'s reply

Does the *C* submit a revised quotation?

NO REVISED QUOTATION RECEIVED

62.4 If none is received, the *E* assesses the CE and notifies the assessment

FC 63 Assessing CEs

Does the *E* agree with a quotation?

Does the *E* agree with the revised quotation?

If the *E* does not agree with the revised quotation the *E* assesses the CE and notifies the assessment

EMPLOYER DISAGREES WITH REVISED QUOTATION

FC 13 Notification by *E*

The period for reply is stated in the CD

REPLY TO OTHER COMPENSATION EVENTS

TIMELY REPLY?

Does the *E* reply within the time allowed?

FC 61 Notifying CE Late reply 60.1(4)

62.3 The *E* replies within two weeks of the *C*'s submission accepting or disagreeing with the quotation

Does the *E* satisfy his assessment within the *period for reply*?

FC 60 Notifying CE Late reply 60.1(4)

TIMELY REPLY?

Finish

A Sheet 1

Does the *C* provide a quotation a time?

CONTRACTOR DOES NOT PROVIDE QUOTATION

62.2 If the *C* does not provide a quotation for a compensation event within the time allowed, the *E* assesses the CE and notifies the *C* of his assessment

FC 63 Assessing CEs

Flow chart 62 Sheet 2 of 2
Quotations for compensation events

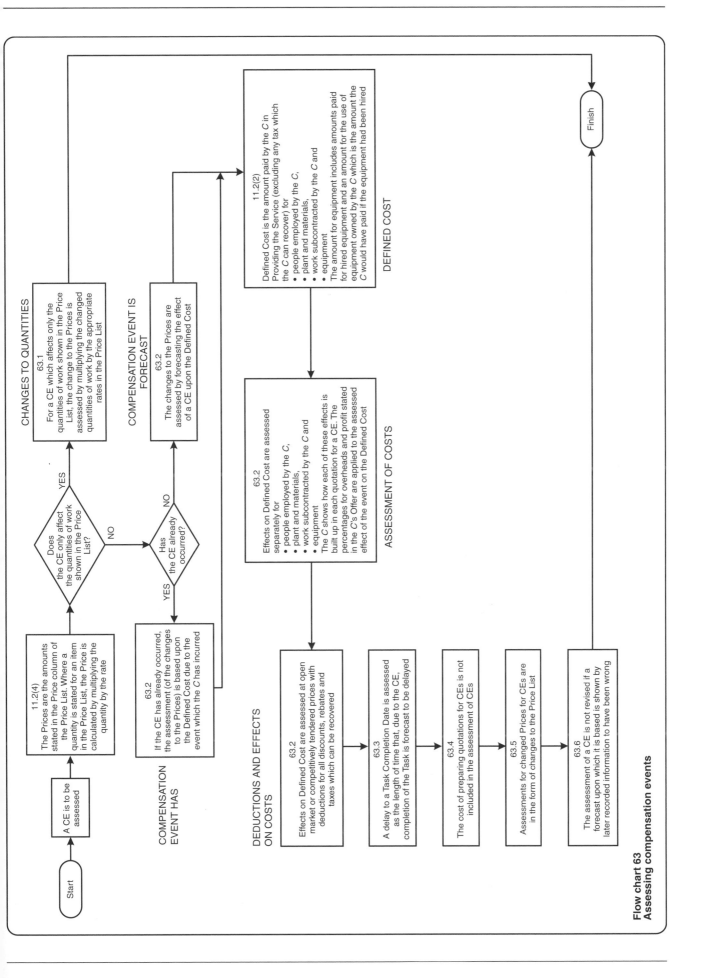

Flow chart 63
Assessing compensation events

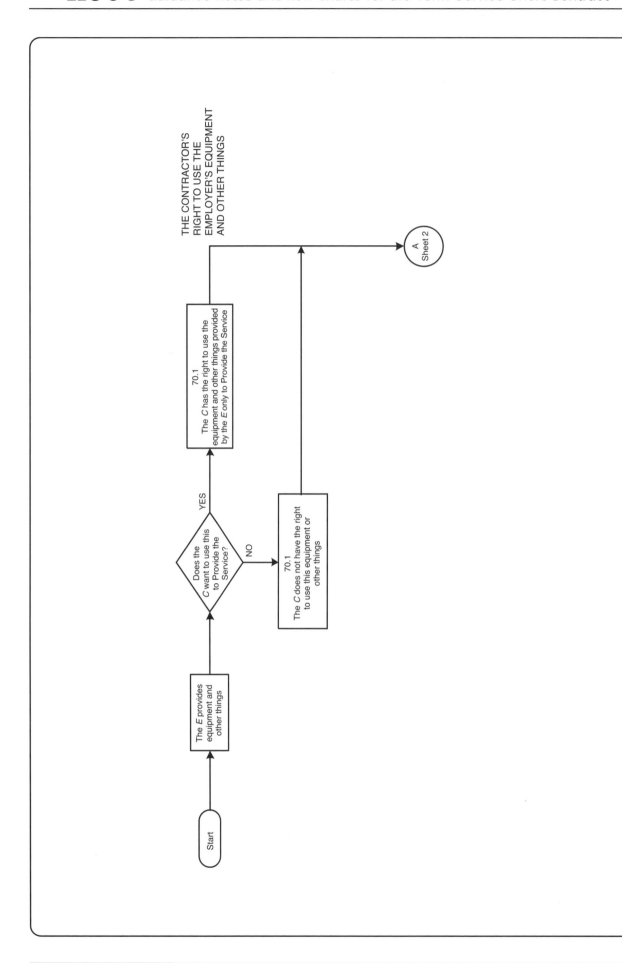

THE CONTRACTOR'S RIGHT TO USE THE EMPLOYER'S EQUIPMENT AND OTHER THINGS

Start

The *E* provides equipment and other things

Does the *C* want to use this to Provide the Service?

YES

70.1
The *C* has the right to use the equipment and other things provided by the *E* only to Provide the Service

NO

70.1
The *C* does not have the right to use this equipment or other things

A
Sheet 2

Flow chart 70 Sheet 1 of 2
The Parties' use of equipment and things

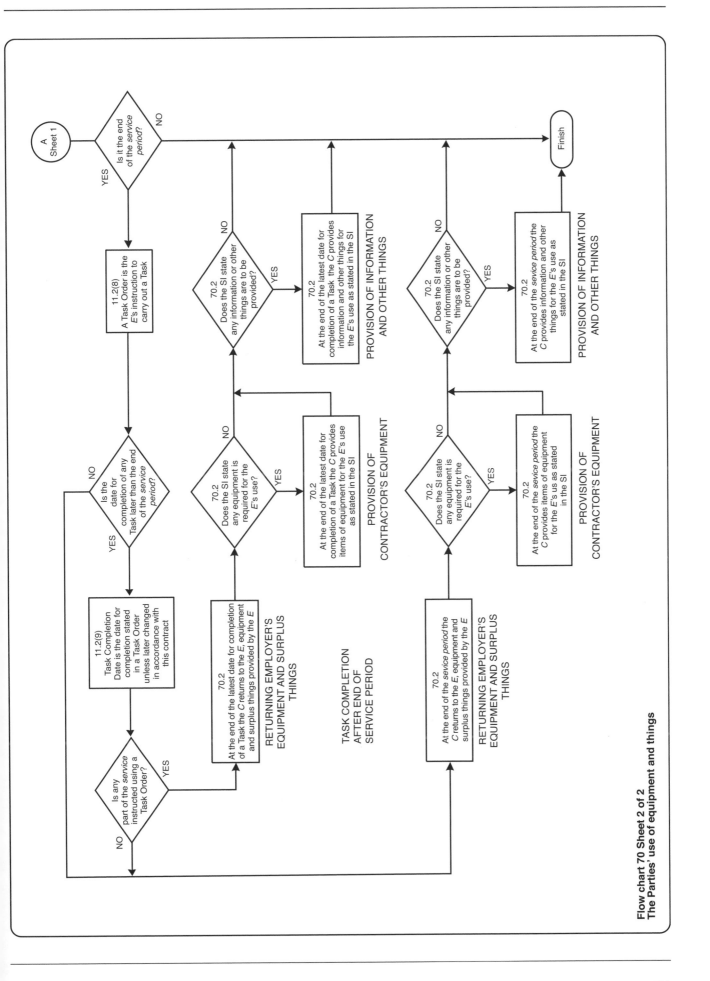

A Sheet 1

Is it the end of the *service period*?
— YES →
— NO →

11.2(8)
A Task Order is the *E*'s instruction to carry out a Task

Is the date for completion of any Task later than the end of the *service period*?
— NO
— YES

11.2(9)
Task Completion Date is the date for completion stated in a Task Order unless later changed in accordance with this contract

Is any part of the *service* instructed using a Task Order?
— NO
— YES

70.2
Does the SI state any information or other things are to be provided?
— NO
— YES

70.2
At the end of the latest date for completion of a Task the *C* provides information and other things for the *E*'s use as stated in the SI

PROVISION OF INFORMATION AND OTHER THINGS

70.2
Does the SI state any equipment is required for the *E*'s use?
— NO
— YES

70.2
At the end of the latest date for completion of a Task the *C* provides items of equipment for the *E*'s use as stated in the SI

PROVISION OF CONTRACTOR'S EQUIPMENT

70.2
At the end of the latest date for completion of a Task the *C* returns to the *E*, equipment and surplus things provided by the *E*

RETURNING EMPLOYER'S EQUIPMENT AND SURPLUS THINGS

TASK COMPLETION AFTER END OF SERVICE PERIOD

70.2
Does the SI state any information or other things are to be provided?
— NO
— YES

70.2
At the end of the *sevice period* the *C* provides information and other things for the *E*'s use as stated in the SI

PROVISION OF INFORMATION AND OTHER THINGS

70.2
Does the SI state any equipment is required for the *E*'s use?
— NO
— YES

70.2
At the end of the *sevice period* the *C* provides items of equipment for the *E*'s us as stated in the SI

PROVISION OF CONTRACTOR'S EQUIPMENT

70.2
At the end of the *sevice period* the *C* returns to the *E*, equipment and surplus things provided by the *E*

RETURNING EMPLOYER'S EQUIPMENT AND SURPLUS THINGS

Finish

Flow chart 70 Sheet 2 of 2
The Parties' use of equipment and things

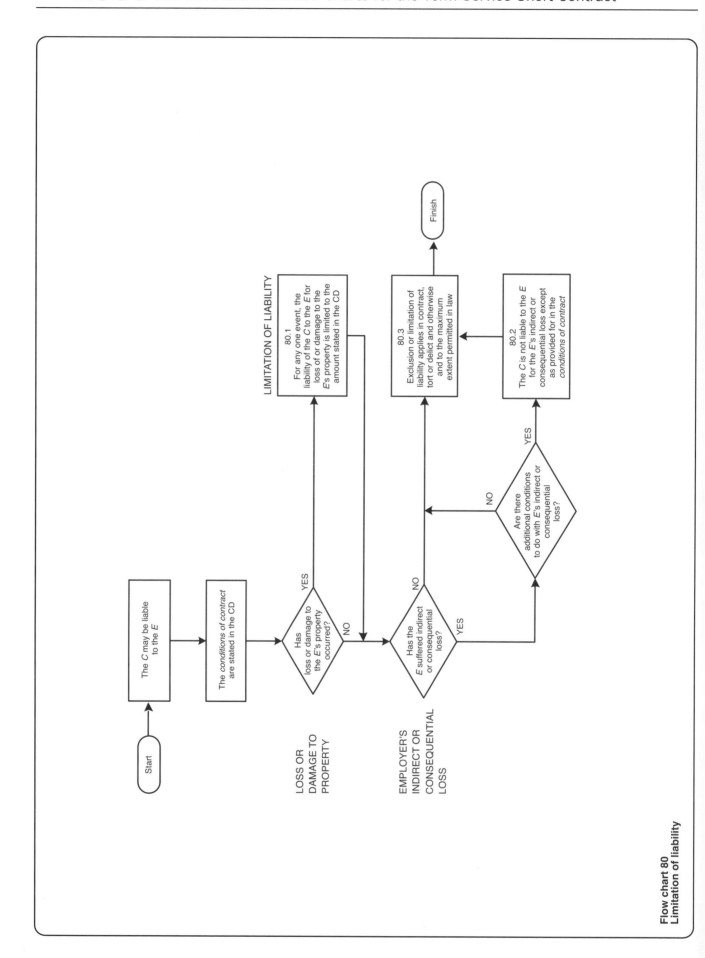

Flow chart 80
Limitation of liability

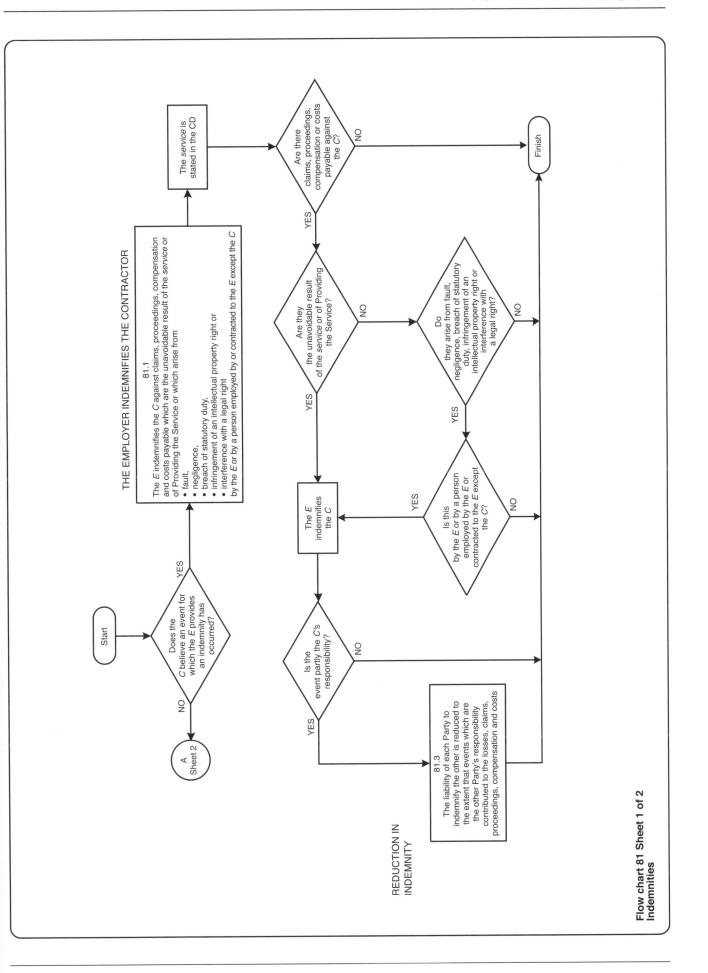

THE EMPLOYER INDEMNIFIES THE CONTRACTOR

81.1

The *E* indemnifies the *C* against claims, proceedings, compensation and costs payable which are the unavoidable result of the *service* or of Providing the Service or which arise from

- fault,
- negligence,
- breach of statutory duty,
- infringement of an intellectual property right or
- interference with a legal right

by the *E* or by a person employed by or contracted to the *E* except the *C*

The *service* is stated in the CD

Start

Does the *C* believe an event for which the *E* provides an indemnity has occurred?

YES → NO

A
Sheet 2

Are there claims, proceedings, compensation or costs payable against the *C*?

YES / NO

Are they the unavoidable result of the *service* or of Providing the Service?

YES / NO

Do they arise from fault, negligence, breach of statutory duty, infringement of an intellectual property right or interference with a legal right?

YES / NO

The *E* indemnifies the *C*

Is this by the *E* or by a person employed by the *E* or contracted to the *E* except the *C*?

YES / NO

Is the event partly the *C*'s responsibility?

YES / NO

Finish

REDUCTION IN INDEMNITY

81.3

The liability of each Party to indemnify the other is reduced to the extent that events which are the other Party's responsibility contributed to the losses, claims, proceedings, compensation and costs

Flow chart 81 Sheet 1 of 2
Indemnities

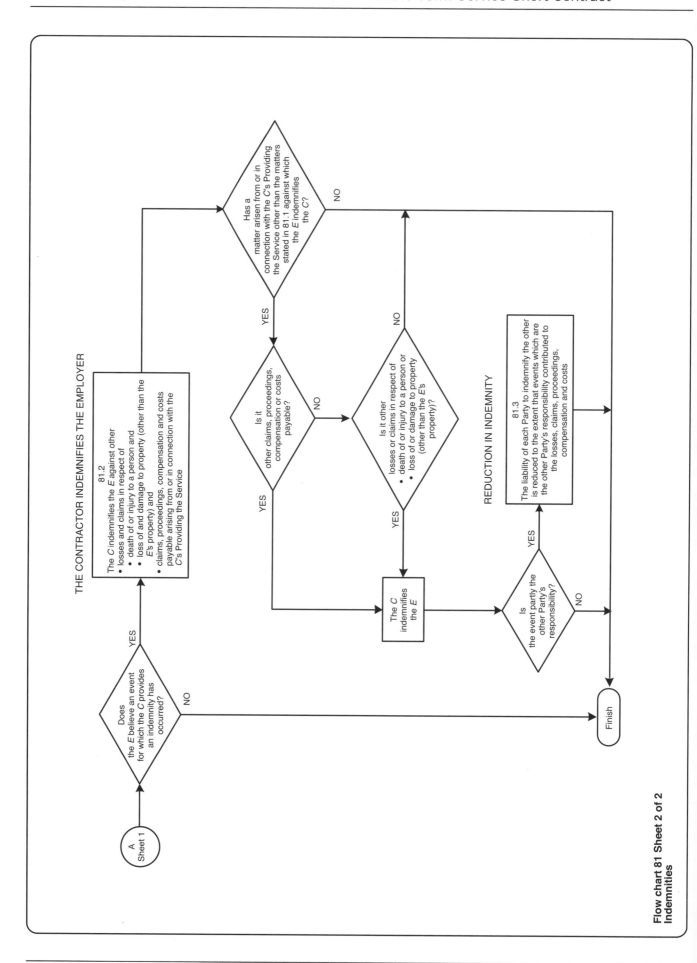

THE CONTRACTOR INDEMNIFIES THE EMPLOYER

81.2
The *C* indemnifies the *E* against other
- losses and claims in respect of
  - death of or injury to a person and
  - loss of and damage to property (other than the *E*'s property) and
- claims, proceedings, compensation and costs payable arising from or in connection with the *C*'s Providing the Service

Does the *E* believe an event for which the *C* provides an indemnity has occurred?

A Sheet 1

YES / NO

Has a matter arisen from or in connection with the *C*'s Providing the Service other than the matters stated in 81.1 against which the *E* indemnifies the *C*?

YES / NO

Is it other claims, proceedings, compensation or costs payable?

YES / NO

Is it other
- losses or claims in respect of
  - death of or injury to a person or
  - loss of or damage to property (other than the *E*'s property)?

YES / NO

The *C* indemnifies the *E*

REDUCTION IN INDEMNITY

81.3
The liability of each Party to indemnify the other is reduced to the extent that events which are the other Party's responsibility contributed to the losses, claims, proceedings, compensation and costs

Is the event partly the other Party's responsibility?

YES / NO

Finish

Flow chart 81 Sheet 2 of 2
Indemnities

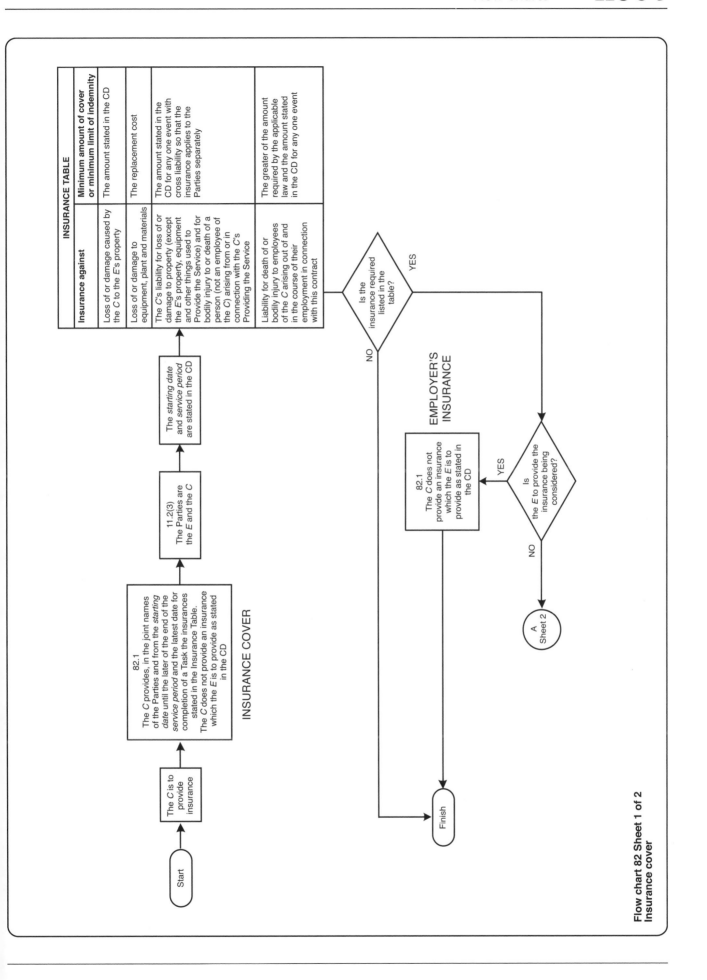

INSURANCE TABLE

Insurance against	Minimum amount of cover or minimum limit of indemnity
Loss of or damage caused by the C to the E's property	The amount stated in the CD
Loss of or damage to equipment, plant and materials	The replacement cost
The C's liability for loss of or damage to property (except the E's property, equipment and other things used to Provide the Service) and for bodily injury to or death of a person (not an employee of the C) arising from or in connection with the C's Providing the Service	The amount stated in the CD for any one event with cross liability so that the insurance applies to the Parties separately
Liability for death of or bodily injury to employees of the C arising out of and in the course of their employment in connection with this contract	The greater of the amount required by the applicable law and the amount stated in the CD for any one event

INSURANCE COVER

Start

The C is to provide insurance

82.1
The C provides, in the joint names of the Parties and from the *starting date* until the later of the end of the *service period* and the latest date for completion of a Task the insurances stated in the Insurance Table. The C does not provide an insurance which the E is to provide as stated in the CD

11.2(3)
The Parties are the E and the C

The *starting date* and *service period* are stated in the CD

Is the insurance required listed in the table?

NO → Finish

YES

EMPLOYER'S INSURANCE

Is the E to provide the insurance being considered?

NO → A Sheet 2

YES

82.1
The C does not provide an insurance which the E is to provide as stated in the CD

Finish

Flow chart 82 Sheet 1 of 2
Insurance cover

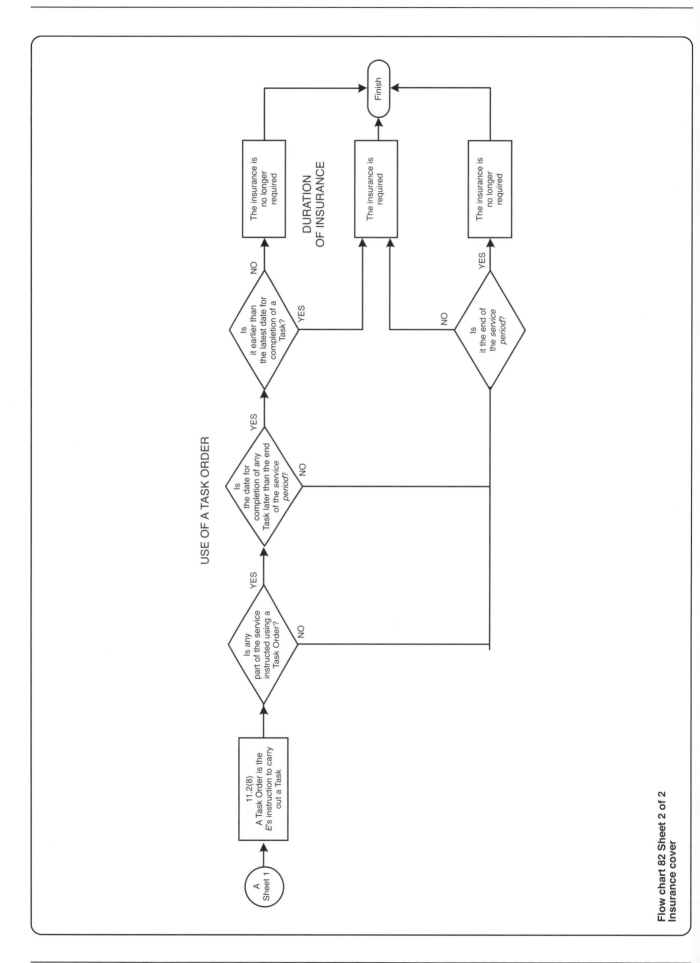

USE OF A TASK ORDER

DURATION OF INSURANCE

A Sheet 1

11.2(8)
A Task Order is the E's instruction to carry out a Task

Is any part of the service instructed using a Task Order?

Is the date for completion of any Task later than the end of the *service period*?

Is it earlier than the latest date for completion of a Task?

Is it the end of the *service period*?

The insurance is no longer required

The insurance is required

The insurance is no longer required

Finish

Flow chart 82 Sheet 2 of 2
Insurance cover

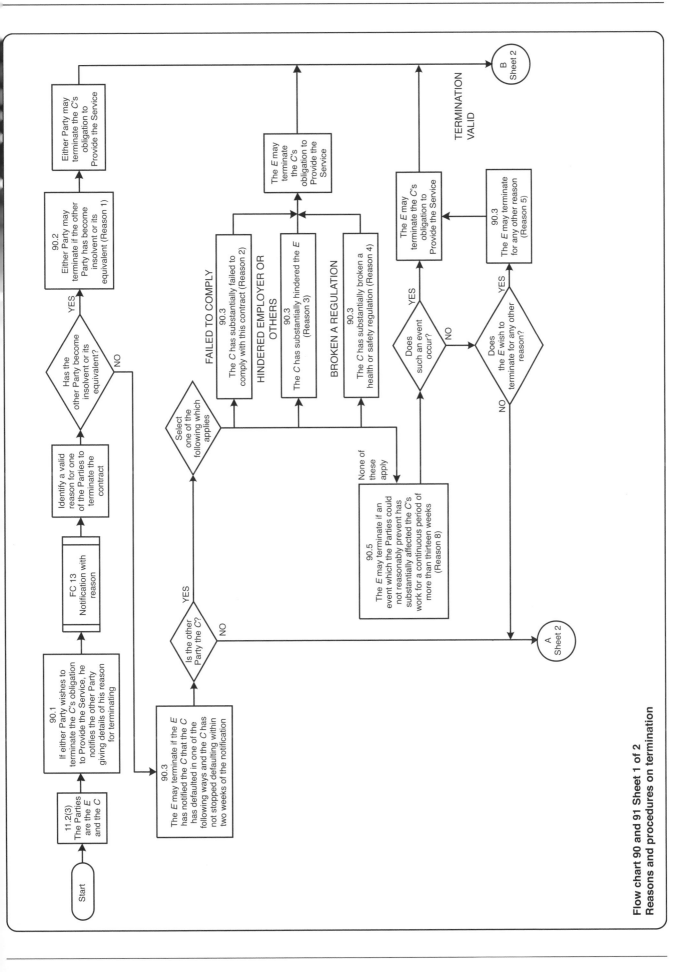

Start

11.2(3)
The Parties are the *E* and the *C*

90.1
If either Party wishes to terminate the *C*'s obligation to Provide the Service, he notifies the other Party giving details of his reason for terminating

FC 13
Notification with reason

Identify a valid reason for one of the Parties to terminate the contract

Has the other Party become insolvent or its equivalent? — YES →

90.2
Either Party may terminate if the other Party has become insolvent or its equivalent (Reason 1)

Either Party may terminate the *C*'s obligation to Provide the Service

NO →

90.3
The *E* may terminate if the *E* has notified the *C* that the *C* has defaulted in one of the following ways and the *C* has not stopped defaulting within two weeks of the notification

Is the other Party the *C*? — YES → / NO →

Select one of the following which applies

FAILED TO COMPLY

90.3
The *C* has substantially failed to comply with this contract (Reason 2)

HINDERED EMPLOYER OR OTHERS

90.3
The *C* has substantially hindered the *E* (Reason 3)

BROKEN A REGULATION

90.3
The *C* has substantially broken a health or safety regulation (Reason 4)

The *E* may terminate the *C*'s obligation to Provide the Service

None of these apply

90.5
The *E* may terminate if an event which the Parties could not reasonably prevent has substantially affected the *C*'s work for a continuous period of more than thirteen weeks (Reason 8)

Does such an event occur? — YES → / NO →

The *E* may terminate the *C*'s obligation to Provide the Service

Does the *E* wish to terminate for any other reason? — YES → / NO →

90.3
The *E* may terminate for any other reason (Reason 5)

TERMINATION VALID

B Sheet 2

A Sheet 2

Flow chart 90 and 91 Sheet 1 of 2
Reasons and procedures on termination

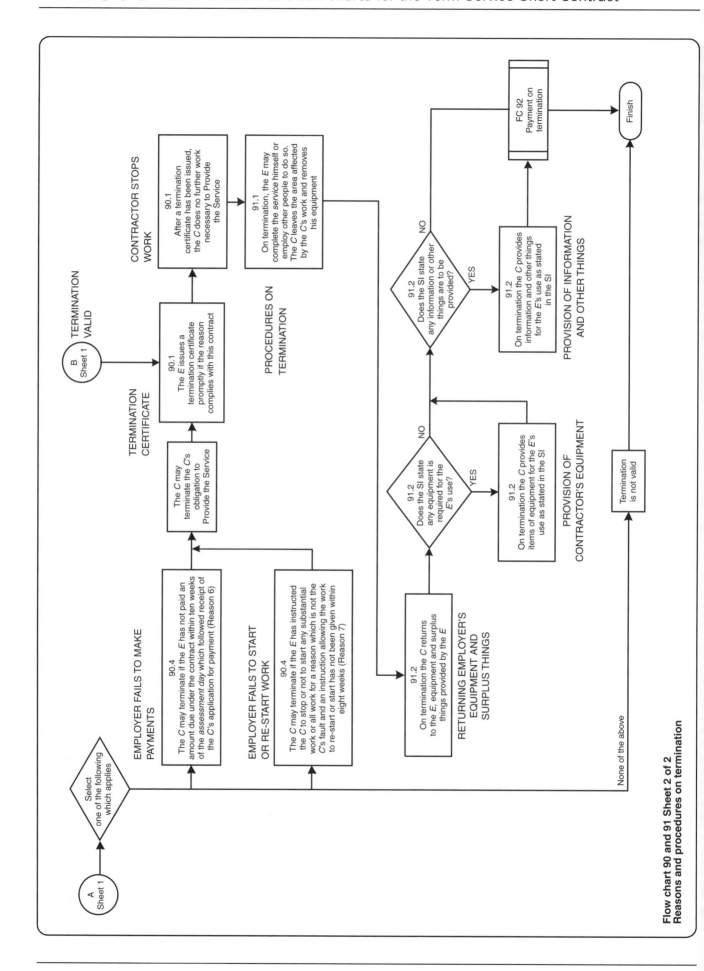

A Sheet 1

Select one of the following which applies

EMPLOYER FAILS TO MAKE PAYMENTS

90.4
The *C* may terminate if the *E* has not paid an amount due under the contract within ten weeks of the *assessment day* which followed receipt of the *C*'s application for payment (Reason 6)

EMPLOYER FAILS TO START OR RE-START WORK

90.4
The *C* may terminate if the *E* has instructed the *C* to stop or not to start any substantial work or all work for a reason which is not the *C*'s fault and an instruction allowing the work to re-start or start has not been given within eight weeks (Reason 7)

B Sheet 1 — TERMINATION VALID

TERMINATION CERTIFICATE

90.1
The *C* may terminate the *C*'s obligation to Provide the Service

90.1
The *E* issues a termination certificate promptly if the reason complies with this contract

CONTRACTOR STOPS WORK

90.1
After a termination certificate has been issued, the *C* does no further work necessary to Provide the Service

91.1
On termination, the *E* may complete the *service* himself or employ other people to do so. The *C* leaves the area affected by the *C*'s work and removes his equipment

PROCEDURES ON TERMINATION

91.2
On termination the *C* returns to the *E*, equipment and surplus things provided by the *E*

RETURNING EMPLOYER'S EQUIPMENT AND SURPLUS THINGS

91.2
Does the SI state any equipment is required for the *E*'s use?

YES → 91.2 On termination the *C* provides items of equipment for the *E*'s use as stated in the SI

NO

PROVISION OF CONTRACTOR'S EQUIPMENT

91.2
Does the SI state any information or other things are to be provided?

YES → 91.2 On termination the *C* provides information and other things for the *E*'s use as stated in the SI

NO

PROVISION OF INFORMATION AND OTHER THINGS

FC 92
Payment on termination

Finish

None of the above → Termination is not valid

Flow chart 90 and 91 Sheet 2 of 2
Reasons and procedures on termination

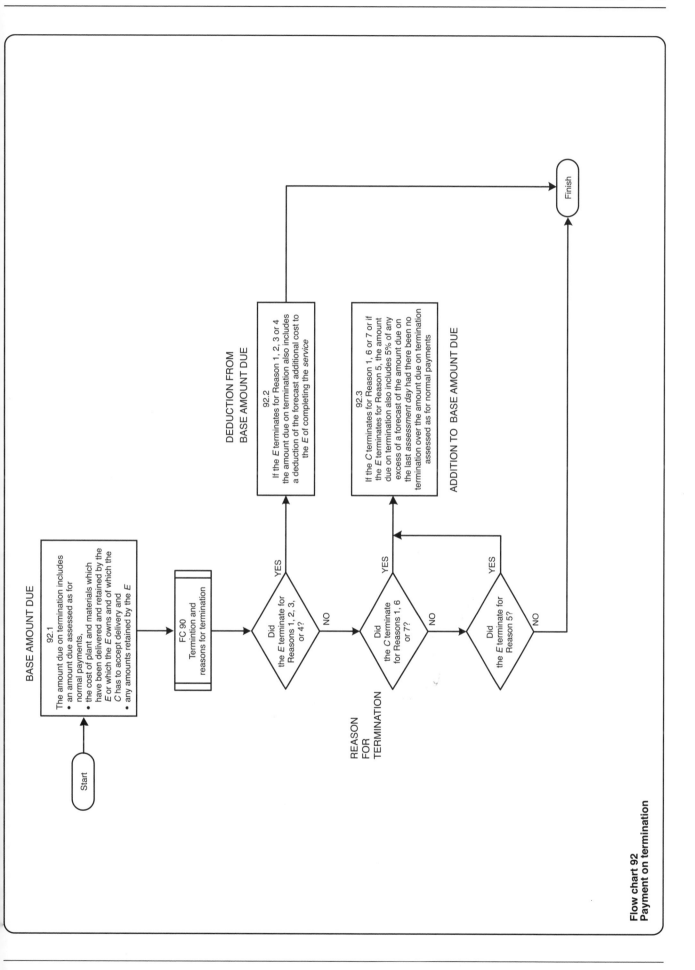

BASE AMOUNT DUE

Start

92.1
The amount due on termination includes
• an amount due assessed as for normal payments,
• the cost of plant and materials which have been delivered and retained by the *E* or which the *E* owns and of which the *C* has to accept delivery and
• any amounts retained by the *E*

FC 90
Termintion and reasons for termination

Did the *E* terminate for Reasons 1, 2, 3, or 4?

REASON FOR TERMINATION

Did the *C* terminate for Reasons 1, 6 or 7?

Did the *E* terminate for Reason 5?

YES

NO

YES

NO

YES

NO

DEDUCTION FROM BASE AMOUNT DUE

92.2
If the *E* terminates for Reason 1, 2, 3 or 4 the amount due on termination also includes a deduction of the forecast additional cost to the *E* of completing the *service*

92.3
If the *C* terminates for Reason 1, 6 or 7 or if the *E* terminates for Reason 5, the amount due on termination also includes 5% of any excess of a forecast of the amount due on the last *assessment day* had there been no termination over the amount due on termination assessed as for normal payments

ADDITION TO BASE AMOUNT DUE

Finish

Flow chart 92
Payment on termination

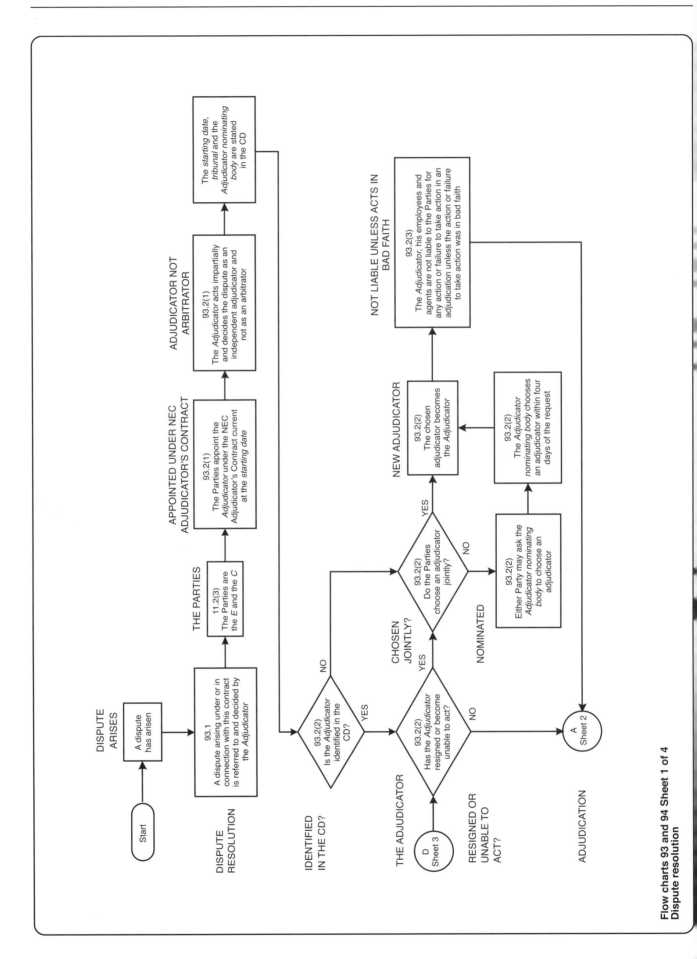

Flow charts 93 and 94 Sheet 1 of 4
Dispute resolution

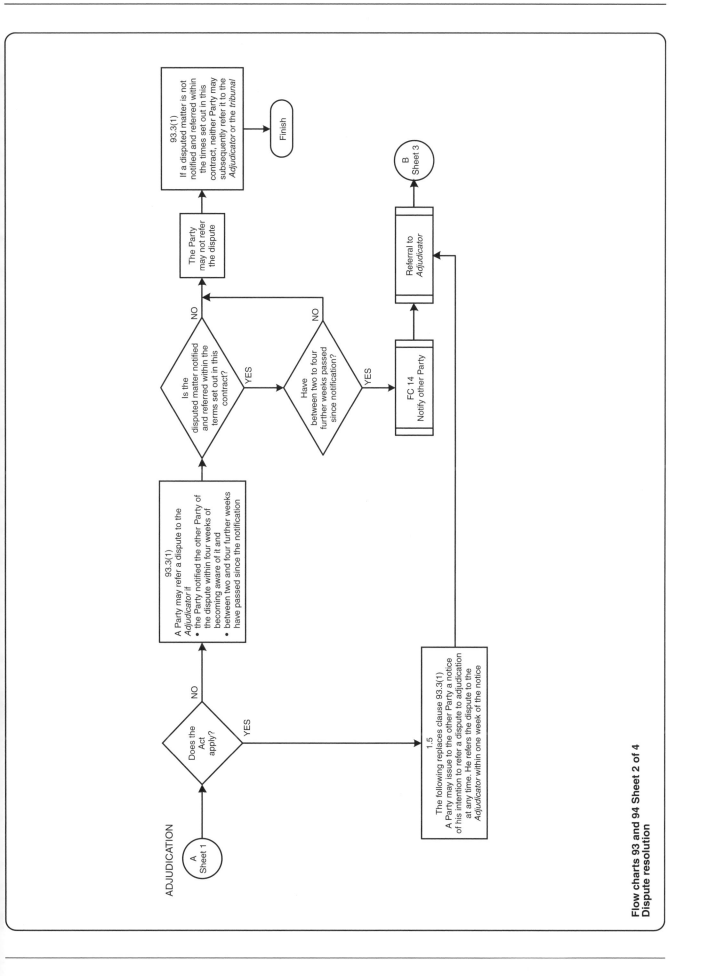

ADJUDICATION

A
Sheet 1

Does the Act apply?

NO →

YES →

93.3(1)
A Party may refer a dispute to the *Adjudicator* if
• the Party notified the other Party of the dispute within four weeks of becoming aware of it and
• between two and four further weeks have passed since the notification

Is the disputed matter notified and referred within the terms set out in this contract?

NO →

YES →

The Party may not refer the dispute

93.3(1)
If a disputed matter is not notified and referred within the times set out in this contract, neither Party may subsequently refer it to the *Adjudicator* or the *tribunal*

Finish

Have between two to four further weeks passed since notification?

NO →

YES →

FC 14
Notify other Party

Referral to *Adjudicator*

B
Sheet 3

1.5
The following replaces clause 93.3(1)
A Party may issue to the other Party a notice of his intention to refer a dispute to adjudication at any time. He refers the dispute to the *Adjudicator* within one week of the notice

Flow charts 93 and 94 Sheet 2 of 4
Dispute resolution

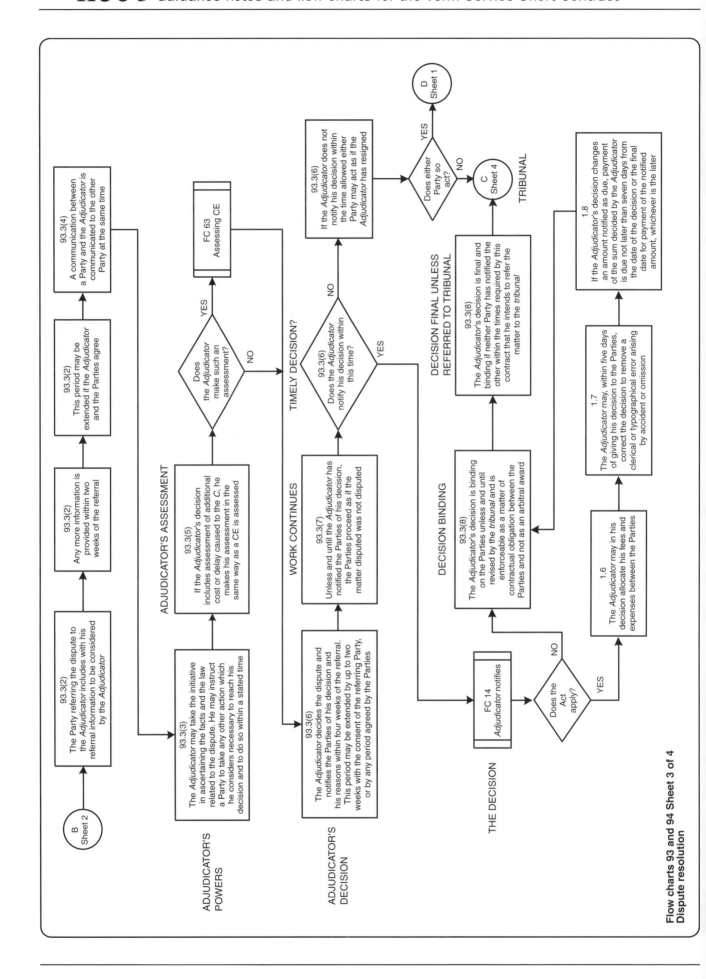

ADJUDICATOR'S POWERS

93.3(3)
The *Adjudicator* may take the initiative in ascertaining the facts and the law related to the dispute. He may instruct a Party to take any other action which he considers necessary to reach his decision and to do so within a stated time

B
Sheet 2

93.3(2)
The Party referring the dispute to the *Adjudicator* includes with his referral information to be considered by the *Adjudicator*

93.3(2)
Any more information is provided within two weeks of the referral

93.3(2)
This period may be extended if the *Adjudicator* and the Parties agree

93.3(4)
A communication between a Party and the *Adjudicator* is communicated to the other Party at the same time

ADJUDICATOR'S ASSESSMENT

93.3(5)
If the *Adjudicator's* decision includes assessment of additional cost or delay caused to the C, he makes his assessment in the same way as a CE is assessed

Does the *Adjudicator* make such an assessment?

YES → FC 63 Assessing CE

NO

ADJUDICATOR'S DECISION

93.3(6)
The *Adjudicator* decides the dispute and notifies the Parties of his decision and his reasons within four weeks of the referral. This period may be extended by up to two weeks with the consent of the referring Party, or by any period agreed by the Parties

WORK CONTINUES

93.3(7)
Unless and until the *Adjudicator* has notified the Parties of his decision, the Parties proceed as if the matter disputed was not disputed

TIMELY DECISION?

93.3(6)
Does the *Adjudicator* notify his decision within this time?

NO → **93.3(6)** If the *Adjudicator* does not notify his decision within the time allowed either Party may act as if the *Adjudicator* has resigned

YES

Does either Party so act?

YES → D Sheet 1

NO → C Sheet 4

TRIBUNAL

THE DECISION

FC 14 *Adjudicator* notifies

Does the Act apply?

NO

YES → **1.6** The *Adjudicator* may in his decision allocate his fees and expenses between the Parties

DECISION BINDING

93.3(8)
The *Adjudicator's* decision is binding on the Parties unless and until revised by the *tribunal* and is enforceable as a matter of contractual obligation between the Parties and not as an arbitral award

DECISION FINAL UNLESS REFERRED TO TRIBUNAL

93.3(8)
The *Adjudicator's* decision is final and binding if neither Party has notified the other within the times required by this contract that he intends to refer the matter to the *tribunal*

1.7 The *Adjudicator* may, within five days of giving his decision to the Parties, correct the decision to remove a clerical or typographical error arising by accident or omission

1.8 If the *Adjudicator's* decision changes an amount notified as due, payment of the sum decided by the *Adjudicator* is due not later than seven days from the date of the decision or the final date for payment of the notified amount, whichever is the later

Flow charts 93 and 94 Sheet 3 of 4
Dispute resolution

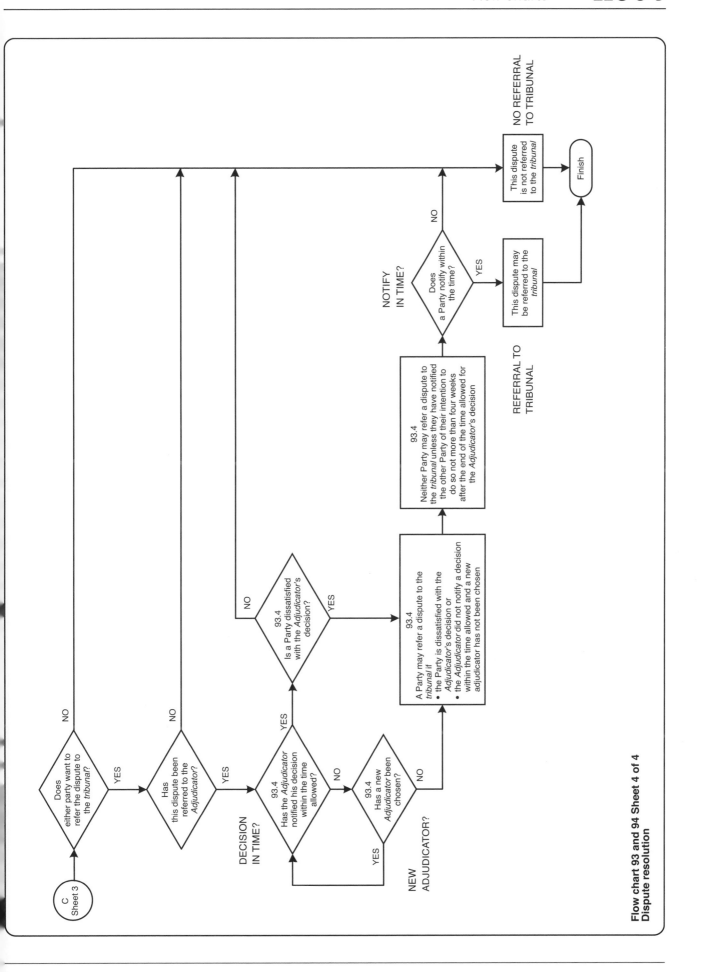

Flow chart 93 and 94 Sheet 4 of 4
Dispute resolution